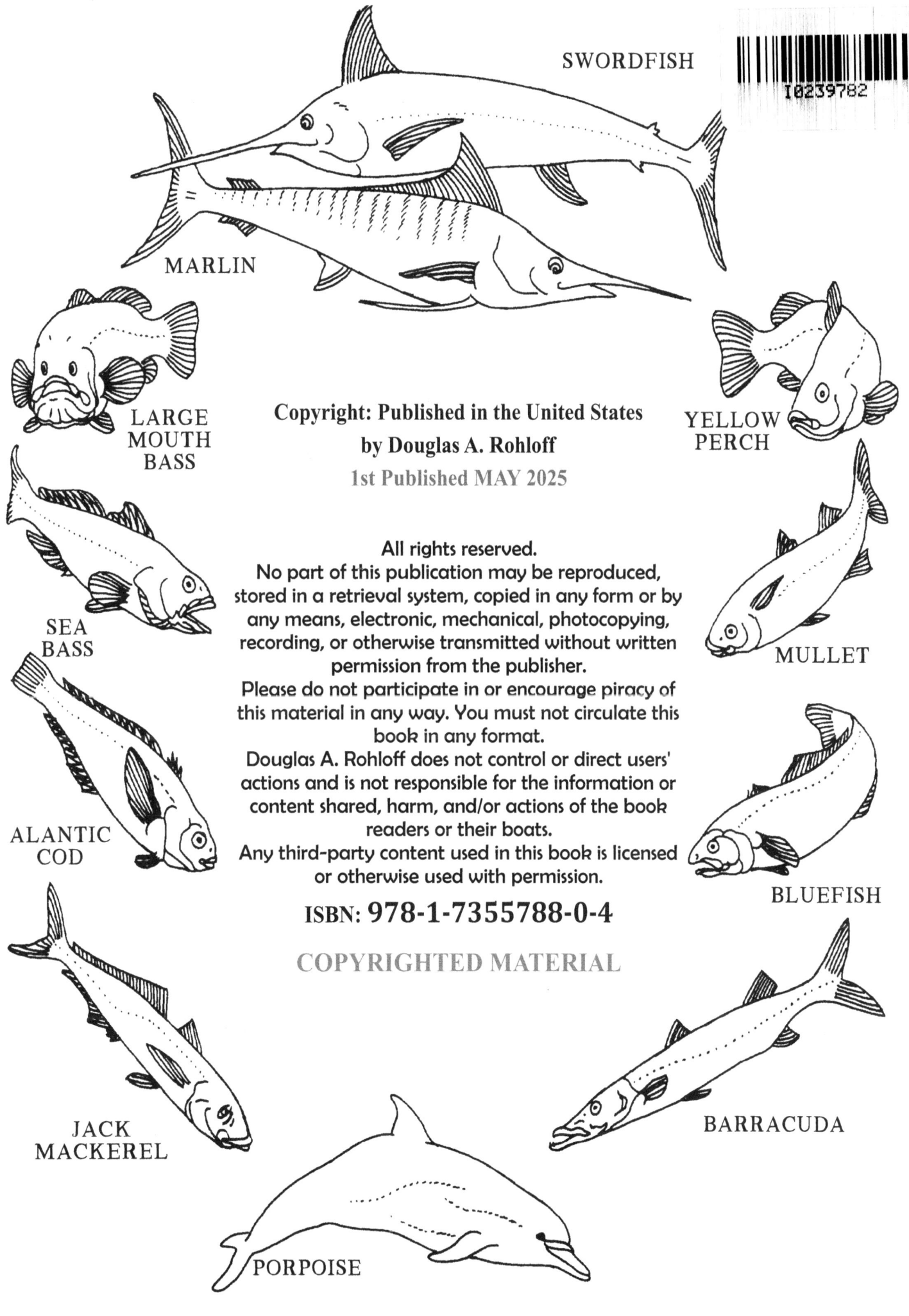

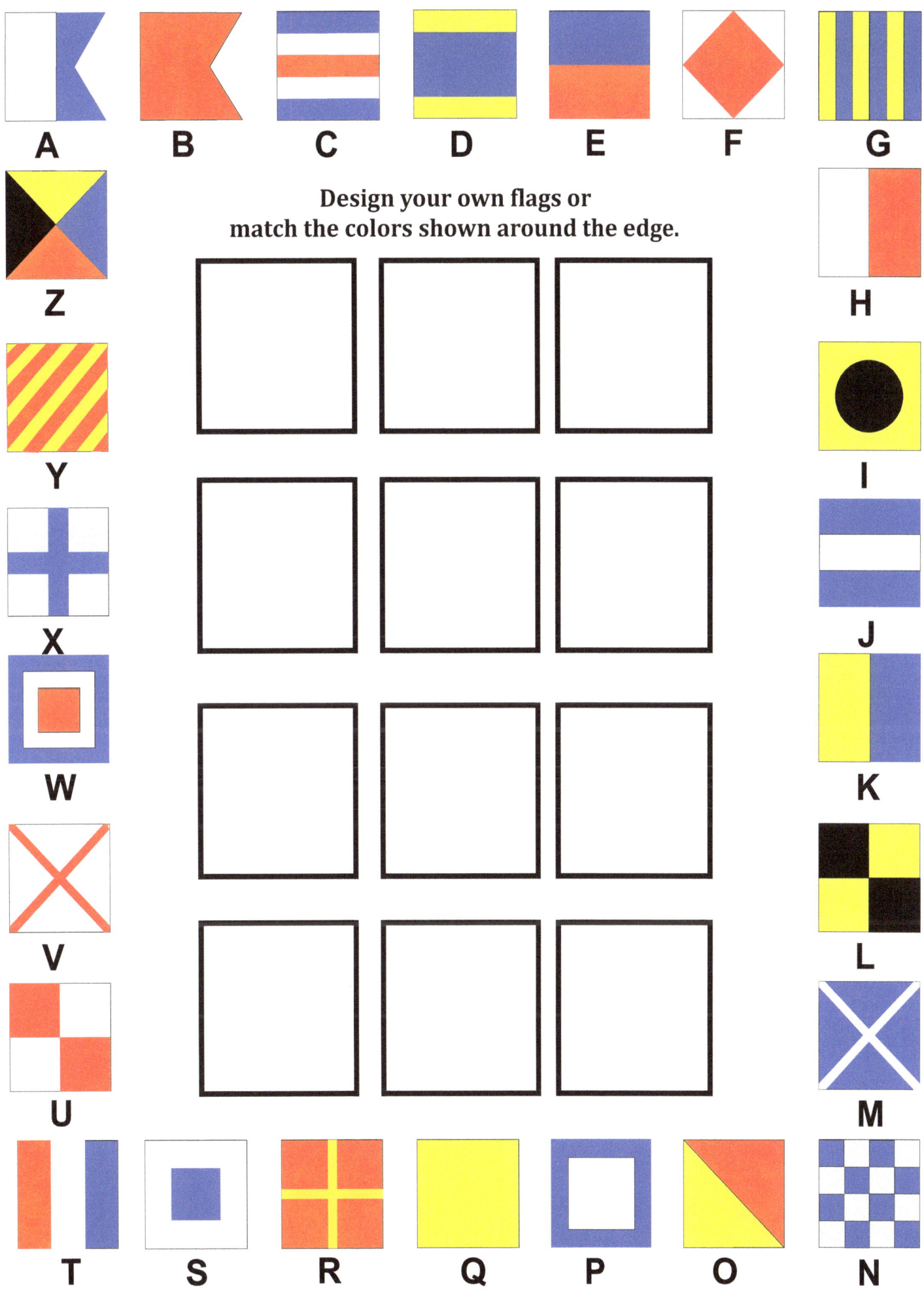

Table Of Contents

This Book Belongs To..2
    Ownership page with sketch/doodle area

Table of Contents..4
    You are here! Organized layout for your boat naming journey.

Preface: Hoist the Sails..6
    A welcome message to get you excited about the adventure ahead.

A Brief History of Boat Naming...............................8
    Global and U.S. traditions, famous names, and folklore.

Boat Naming Traditions & Superstitions.................10
    Ceremonies, taboos, and renaming rituals.

What's in a Name?...12
    Worksheet-style brainstorming activity.

The Boat Name Process..17
    A-to-Z guide from idea to install.

Lettering 101..24
    Font selection, spacing, and readability tips.

Design Ideas & Examples.......................................31
    Visual samples, creative sparks, and layout sketches.

Choosing Boat Name Colors...................................32
    Psychology of color, matching tips, and what works on water.

Is It Bad Luck to Remove a Boat Name?..................46
The myths and truths behind renaming.

How to Remove a Boat Name..................47
Step-by-step removal process for clean results.

DIY Boat Name Installation..................52
Tools, techniques, tips, and troubleshooting.

Registration Numbers & Requirements..................58
USCG plaque info, state guidelines, size rules.

Port Names & Hailing Ports..................62
What they are, where they go, and how to pick one.

Notes & Doodles..................68
Blank and lined pages for your thoughts, drawings, or custom names.

Accessories to Name Too!..................78
Life rings, tiki bar signs, and more.

The Boat Name Gallery..................92
A chosen collection of boat name installs, layouts and inspiration.

Solutions to Puzzles & Games..................105
Answers for fun challenges placed throughout the book.

Hoist the Sails

Ahoy, Captain, fellow Seafarers, and Maritime Enthusiasts!

Welcome aboard this exciting journey into the world of boat naming! Whether you're an experienced sailor, a landlubber dreaming of the open seas, or somewhere in between, this book will be your guide to navigating the fun and creative process of naming your boat and exploring the nautical decor that comes with it.

As a busy graphic designer, I've always wanted to write this book but never found the time. However, I realized that many boat owners needed help with one simple, yet essential task—naming their boats. Many captains and their mates were unsure where to start, and that's where I came in. After receiving numerous requests for a practical guide, I decided to create a workbook that focuses on the how-to, rather than the history of boat naming. By asking a few questions about their lifestyle and intentions for their boat, I could suggest fonts and designs that suited their adventures. This led to the creation of my Boat Name Form, which many found easy to use.

As a passionate boat owner and lover of all things maritime, I've experienced the thrill of naming and designing the perfect boat name, and the pride that comes with it. Naming a boat isn't just about words on the hull—it's about capturing the spirit of the vessel and the adventure ahead.

In this book, I share the knowledge and insights I've gathered over the years. Whether you're looking for inspiration, practical advice on designing and installing boat names, or simply want to appreciate the rich tradition of boat naming, you'll find it here.

You'll explore the fascinating lore and superstitions surrounding boat names, uncover the stories behind iconic vessels in maritime history, and discover tips for brainstorming creative ideas. Along the way, I'll guide you through the process of selecting the right design, navigating legal considerations, and bringing your boat name to life.

This book isn't just about practical tips; it's also a celebration of the unique bond between boat and owner, and the camaraderie of the boating community. It's a testament to the enduring allure of the sea and the joy of exploring the great unknown.

So, hoist the sails, unfurl the flag, and join me on this exciting voyage into the art and tradition of boat naming. Whether you're embarking on your first adventure or adding a new chapter to your journey, may this book be your trusted companion.

Fair winds and flowing seas,

Doug A. Rohloff

Set Course for Adventure!

Ahoy, fellow captains, and welcome aboard this thrilling voyage into the captivating realm of boat naming! As we embark on this exhilarating journey together, I extend to you an invitation to cast off the lines and join me as we navigate through the rich tapestry of history, tradition, and innovation that defines the art of boat naming.

For eons, humanity has been drawn to the boundless expanse of the open seas, and vessels of all shapes and sizes have played an integral role in our exploration, trade, and adventures. From the humblest rowboat to the majestic ocean liners, each boat possesses a unique identity, symbolized by its name—a name that encapsulates the aspirations, dreams, and spirit of its owner.

In this chapter, we embark on a voyage into the captivating world of boat naming, where we delve into the timeless traditions, captivating folklore, and contemporary innovations that shape the way we christen our vessels. From the dawn of seafaring to the present day, boat naming has been revered as a cherished ritual, steeped in a sense of pride and ownership.

Yet, boat naming is far more than simply selecting a name—it is an odyssey of self-discovery, creativity, and self-expression. It is about encapsulating the essence of adventure and the thrill of exploration within a single word or phrase, as we set sail into uncharted waters with boundless enthusiasm and joy.

So, hoist the sails, my fellow seafarers, and let us chart a course for adventure together! Whether you are a seasoned mariner with a lifetime of voyages or a landlubber dreaming of the high seas, there is a magical allure to the process of naming a boat—a sense of anticipation, excitement, and endless possibilities that stirs the soul and ignites the imagination.

As we journey through the chapters ahead, I invite you to join me in unraveling the stories, traditions, and inspirations behind some of history's most iconic boat names. Together, we will celebrate the rich diversity of nautical culture and perhaps find inspiration to christen our own vessels with names that echo across the waves.

So, gather your compass, my fellow captains, as we embark on an unforgettable odyssey into the realm of boat naming. Fair winds and following seas beckon us forth to new horizons!

MEET LUCY

At 5 years old, Lucy is not just a golden retriever—she's the heart and soul of our boat naming adventures. With her wagging tail and boundless energy, Lucy brings joy, inspiration, and a touch of canine magic to our creative process. As my faithful companion and trusted confidante, Lucy is more than just a pet—she's my loyal helper and good luck charm for crafting the perfect boat names. So, join us on this journey with Lucy by our side, as we navigate the seas of imagination and embark on unforgettable adventures together!"

Brief History of Boat Naming

Boat naming traces its origins back to ancient civilizations that emerged around 3000 BCE. In ancient Egypt, boats were often named after gods and goddesses, with examples dating back to the early dynastic period (c. 3100–2686 BCE). Similarly, ancient Greek and Roman vessels bore names inspired by mythology, with boat naming practices dating back to the Bronze Age (c. 3000–1200 BCE).

During the Age of Exploration in the 15th to 17th centuries, European explorers embarked on voyages of discovery to chart new territories and establish trade routes. Notable expeditions, such as Christopher Columbus's journey to the Americas in 1492 and Ferdinand Magellan's circumnavigation of the globe from 1519 to 1522, featured ships named after monarchs, sponsors, or symbolic concepts.

In naval history, boat naming became institutionalized during the age of sail in the 17th to 19th centuries. Warships of the Royal Navy and other European navies were often given powerful or intimidating names, with traditions dating back to the Tudor period in England (1485–1603). Battleships, frigates, and other naval vessels bore names that reflected national pride, historical figures, or naval victories.

The 20th century saw the continuation of boat naming traditions alongside innovations in maritime technology and culture. Commercial shipping fleets, luxury liners, and recreational boats adopted naming conventions that reflected changing social norms and aspirations. World War II (1939–1945) witnessed the christening of numerous warships and merchant vessels, many of which bore names that honored fallen heroes and wartime achievements.

Today, boat naming remains a vibrant tradition in maritime communities worldwide, spanning recreational boating, commercial fishing, and luxury yachting. Boat owners continue to draw inspiration from mythology, history, literature, and personal experiences when choosing names for their vessels. Boat naming ceremonies, naming contests, and creative naming conventions continue to enrich the maritime culture, preserving the legacy of this ancient practice into the modern era.

Susie Sea

Why Boat Names Are the Treasure of the Seas

Boat names are more than just words painted on a hull or emblazoned on a flag—they are the treasure chests of the seas, each containing a trove of stories, dreams, and adventures waiting to be unlocked. Like precious gems adorning the crown of a mighty king, boat names add character, charm, and personality to vessels of all shapes and sizes.

Every boat name is a testament to the unique bond between owner and vessel, a reflection of the hopes, aspirations, and passions of those who dare to brave the open waters. Whether it's a playful pun, a nod to nautical tradition, or a heartfelt tribute to a loved one, each name carries with it a piece of its owner's heart, transforming a mere vessel into a cherished companion on the voyage of life.

But the allure of boat names goes beyond mere sentimentality—they are also symbols of adventure, exploration, and discovery. Just as ancient mariners carved their names into the annals of history with each daring voyage, so too do modern-day sailors leave their mark on the world with the names they choose for their vessels. With each stroke of the brush or click of the mouse, they imbue their boats with a sense of identity and purpose, setting sail into the unknown with courage, determination, and a spirit of adventure.

In a world filled with uncertainty and chaos, boat names stand as beacons of hope, guiding sailors through stormy seas and calm waters alike. They are reminders of the joys of exploration, the thrill of discovery, and the beauty of the natural world that surrounds us. Whether seen from afar or up close and personal, a well-chosen boat name has the power to captivate the imagination, spark conversation, and inspire awe in all who behold it.

So, why are boat names the treasure of the seas? Because they are more than just words—they are symbols of courage, creativity, and camaraderie that unite sailors across oceans and continents. They are the keys to unlocking the mysteries of the deep and the treasures that lie within. And above all, they are the heart and soul of every vessel that sails the seven seas, forever etched into the fabric of maritime history as symbols of adventure, exploration, and the indomitable spirit of the human soul.

About Boat Naming Traditions

For centuries, boat names have held significant meaning, from honoring individuals to invoking good fortune at sea. Maritime traditions consider a boat's name more than just identification—it represents protection, identity, and status.

The Superstition of Boat Naming
Sailors have long believed that renaming a boat without a proper ceremony can bring bad luck. According to legend, Poseidon, the god of the sea, records every vessel's name in the "Ledger of the Deep." To rename a boat, one must first remove all traces of the old name and hold a ritual to appease the gods of the sea and winds.

Why Boats are Traditionally Named After Women
Many historic ships bear female names, a practice dating back to ancient times. Some say it's because ships were once dedicated to goddesses, while others believe a boat is like a "mother" that carries and protects its crew. Today, boat owners choose names that reflect personal stories, interests, and aspirations.

The Role of Symbols and Themes in Boat Names
Beyond words, many boat names feature anchors, compasses, waves, and nautical symbols to represent adventure, direction, and strength. A well-designed boat name includes these elements as a representation of the captain's vision on the water.

Your Boat, Your Legacy
Whether naming a boat for the first time or continuing a family tradition, a boat's name tells a story. With custom-designed lettering and graphics, boaters can ensure their vessel stands out with a name that is meaningful and enduring.

About Boat Naming Traditions
Boat names have long carried deep meaning, honoring loved ones or invoking good fortune. They are not just identifiers but symbols of protection, identity, and prestige.

The Superstition of Boat Naming
Sailors believe renaming a boat without a proper ceremony brings bad luck. Legend says Poseidon records every vessel's name in the "Ledger of the Deep." Renaming requires removing all traces of the old name and performing a ritual to appease the sea gods.

Your Boat, Your Legacy
Naming a boat tells a story. Custom-designed lettering and graphics ensure your vessel stands out with a meaningful and lasting name.

"A boat without a name is like a ship without a sail—lost at sea!"
– Unknown

"There is nothing more enticing, disenchanting, and enslaving than the life at sea."
– Joseph Conrad

"Boat names: because 'Ship Happens' doesn't quite cut it."
– Unknown

What's in a Name?
Your Boat's Identity Begins Here

Use this step-by-step worksheet to create a boat name that reflects your lifestyle, passion, or humor. Circle what applies, write in your answers, and let the name come to life.

✸ Step 1: Describe Your Boat
- Boat Type (e.g. Sailboat, Pontoon, Fishing, Cruiser): _____
- Color Scheme or Standout Feature: _____
- Style or Personality (Classic, Sporty, Funky?): _____

✸ Step 2: Capture Your Vibe
- What's the feel?
   (Circle one or write your own)
   Elegant / Chill / Bold / Tropical / Playful / Mysterious / Sentimental / Rugged / Custom: ___
- What's the boat used for? (Fishing, Exploring, Relaxing): _____

✸ Step 3: Personal Touches
- Include family names or initials? _____
- Places you love? _____
- Dates that matter? _____
- Hobbies or lifestyle themes? _____

✸ Step 4: Wordplay & Puns
- Try combining a nautical term with a personal word.
   (Examples: Knot Home, Pier Pressure, Sea Señorita)
- Mashups or double meanings: _____
- Nicknames or phrases you say a lot: _____

Pro Tip: *Try saying your top name ideas out loud to a friend or on the dock!*

✸ Step 5: Draft Your Favorites
Write down your top ideas here:
1. _____
2. _____
3. _____
4. _____
5. _____

Need more space? See "Notes & Doodles" at the back of the book!

✸ Step 6: Test It Out
- Say it out loud. Does it sound right?
- Would it look great on your boat?
- Can people spell and say it easily?
- Does it still make you smile tomorrow?

REMEMBER — MOST OF ALL, HAVE FUN WITH IT.

Naming your boat should feel like part of the adventure, not a chore.
Don't get caught in endless rabbit holes or spend too much energy chasing everyone else's opinion.
The best names come when you stay true to your story, your sense of humor, or your dreams.
Be bold, be playful, and trust that the right name will surface when the time is right.
Enjoy the process — and let it reflect you.

Sometimes all it takes is a little humor to get the ideas flowing.

This playful name generator was originally made for Facebook and Instagram to help captains, families, and dock neighbors crack a smile and kick-start the naming process. It's just for fun — but don't be surprised if something silly sparks the perfect idea. After all, the best names often come when you're not trying too hard. Go ahead, take it for a spin!

What Will Be Your New Boat Name?

	FIRST LETTER OF YOUR FIRST NAME	FIRST LETTER OF YOUR MIDDLE NAME	FIRST LETTER OF YOUR LAST NAME
ABC	THE WILD	DRUNKEN	SEA LOVER
DEF	CAPTAIN	CRAZY	WAVE CHASER
GHI	THE	WEIRD	SHIP POOPER
JKL	THE LAZY	BLUE	FISH KILLER
MNO	THE PRIVATE	MELLOW	FAST RIDER
PQR	CHIEF	SOCIALBLE	ISLAND HOPPER
STU	THE MASTER	WAVY	SUN FINDER
VW	THE MAD	WINDY	SALT DOG
XYZ	THE FLIRTY	NEW	FISH HEAD

Boat NAME Guy   www.BoatNameGuy.com

How to Come Up with a Boat Name

Naming your boat is one of the most exciting parts of ownership.
It's your boat's first impression, its identity, and a reflection of you as the captain.
Here are five solid strategies to help you land on the perfect boat name:

1. Reflect on Your Journey

A boat's name should embody the spirit of its owner and the adventures ahead. Think about the **journeys** you want to take or the **experiences** you cherish most. Whether it's a nod to your love of the sea, a favorite destination, or an aspiration, a name that reflects your journey adds personal meaning.

- **Example:** "Wanderlust" for those who are always chasing new adventures on the open water.
- **Quick Tip:** Ask yourself: **What does boating mean to me?** Is it about **freedom**, **escape**, or **exploration**? Use your answers as inspiration.

2. Use Wordplay or Puns

A fun way to name your boat is to **play with words**. Puns or word combinations make for memorable, light-hearted names that bring smiles to anyone who hears them. This method works best if you're aiming for a name that's **quirky** or **fun**.

- **Example:** "Seas the Day" or "Vitamin Sea" – playful phrases that tie in perfectly with nautical life.
- **Quick Tip:** Think about phrases, sayings, or words with a **sea** twist. **Wordplay** makes your boat name stand out and adds personality.

3. Look to the Sea for Inspiration

Draw inspiration from the **ocean**, **maritime history**, or **sea creatures**. The sea is full of symbolism, and drawing from it ensures that your boat's name will always resonate with the adventure of being on the water. Whether it's a **mythical creature**, **nautical term**, or a **historical figure**, the sea is your playground.

- **Example:** "Poseidon's Pride" or "The Kraken" – powerful names inspired by mythology or natural elements.
- **Quick Tip:** Look at **marine life** or **maritime legends** for inspiration. Incorporating these elements makes your boat feel connected to the vast ocean.

4. Inspiration from People and Places

Sometimes, the best boat names come from the people, places, and experiences that have shaped your life. Think of names that have sentimental value—whether from **family**, **friends**, or **memorable moments**. You can also find inspiration in your **favorite destinations** or places that have special meaning to you. A boat name rooted in people and places brings a personal touch and a deep connection to your boating life.

1. Honor a Loved One

Naming your boat after a **family member**, **friend**, or **pet** is a heartfelt way to commemorate those who have influenced your life. It could be a tribute to a beloved **grandparent**, a **favorite pet**, or someone who inspired your love for the sea.

5. Embrace the Boating Lifestyle

Your boat's name doesn't just represent you—it can also reflect the **boating lifestyle** you embrace. Whether you're a **weekend warrior**, a **cruiser**, or someone who loves the thrill of **racing**, your boat name can embody your passion for the water and the type of adventures you seek.

1. Reflect Your Boating Style

Think about your **boating routine**. Do you prefer cruising along the coast, exploring quiet coves, or racing to the finish line? Your boat name can embody the way you interact with the sea. A **racing-inspired name** or a **cruiser name** will feel more aligned with your boating adventures.

- **Example:** **"Wind Warrior"** (for racers) or **"Endless Horizon"** (for cruisers) – names that reflect your boating passions.
- **Quick Tip:** Consider what part of the **boating lifestyle** resonates most with you. A name that reflects your style will enhance your connection to the boat.

Finding the Perfect Fit

Choosing a boat name should be an exciting, creative process that reflects who you are and what you love about life on the water. By using these three methods—**reflection, wordplay, and the sea**—you're sure to find a name that not only fits your boat but becomes a part of your maritime identity.

Create Your Boat name

Think about your journey, lifestyle, and personality.

Fill in the lines below to brainstorm your boat name.

_____

_____

_____

_____

Some ideas to help inspire you:

Seas the Day | Endless Horizon | Wanderlust

_____

_____

_____

_____

Conclusion:

When naming your boat, look to your **relationships**, **experiences**, and **lifestyle** for inspiration. Whether it's an homage to a person or place, or a reflection of your personal boating style, a name that connects with who you are will make your boat feel like home.

Now that you've brainstormed the perfect name, it's time to bring it to life.

Whether you're replacing an old name or starting fresh,
the next steps are part of the fun —
removing the old lettering (if there is one),
choosing a design, and making it official.

This is where your vision becomes real.
From picking the right font and color
to deciding where and how the name will appear on your boat,
every detail adds to the personality of your vessel.

You might decide to do it all yourself,
or you may want a little help —
that's where people like me (and Lucy, of course) come in.
We help you design it, ship it, and cheer you on
while you bring it to life.

You can create the look on your own
and have it shipped to your door, ready to apply.
Or, if you're feeling confident,
design and install it completely by hand.

Either way, this next chapter will guide you
through the practical parts of the boat name process —
so your final result looks just as great on the water
as it did in your head.

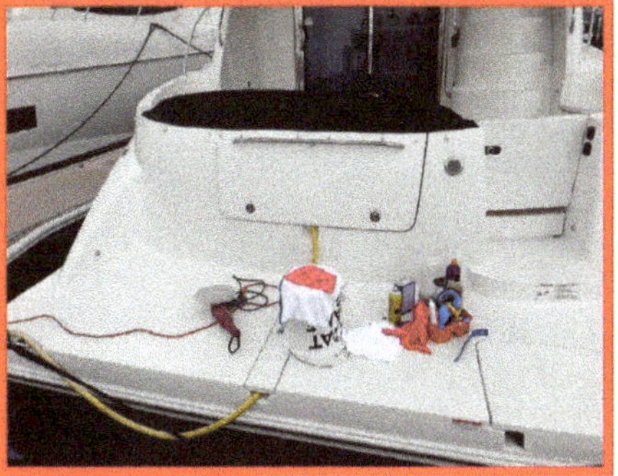

Keep It Short and Shoutable

How to Choose a Name That Looks Good and Sounds Good
When it comes to naming your boat, less is more. A name that's short, sharp, and easy to pronounce could be the difference between a head-turner at the dock and a tongue-twister over the radio.

Stay Under 33 Characters
Most transoms (that's your boat's butt!) can comfortably fit around 20–33 characters. This includes spaces and punctuation. Anything longer risks:
Looking squished or too small
Being hard to read from a distance
Getting cut off in your vinyl layout

Say It Out Loud
Try this: Pretend you're hailing the Coast Guard or calling a friend on Channel 16.
Example:
"Mayday, Mayday — this is Seas the Day, Seas the Day…"
If your name doesn't flow off the tongue, or if it sounds like an emergency ("Help Me" or "Man Down") — time to rethink it.

Avoid Radio Confusion
The U.S. Coast Guard and marine radio operators recommend names that are:
Phonetically clear
Not easily confused with distress calls (e.g., SOS, Mayday, Fire)
Not offensive or misleading

Boat Name Quick Test
Ask yourself:
Is it under 33 characters?
Can I say it clearly three times in a row on a radio?
Would someone else instantly know how to spell it if they heard it once?
Does it avoid terms that could trigger panic or confusion?

Shorter names usually look better in bold or stylized lettering — they give your designer (or you) more room to play.

CAPTAIN'S ORDERS:
You must laugh at least once while naming your boat. That's non-negotiable. ⚓

Dock Talk:
If your boat name makes someone giggle at the ramp, you're doing something right.

Name it like you mean it
and then wear it like a tattoo on fiberglass.

Lucy's Rule #1:
No boring boat names. Ever.
(She'll judge you from the dock.)

Chart Your Boat's Name Placement

Puzzle Directions:
Ahoy, boat lovers! Ready to have some fun and learn where to place your boat's name? In this puzzle, you will match the parts of the boat with the correct location for where the boat name could go. Take a look at the boat parts listed on the left, and match each one

"Not just pretty — placement matters!"

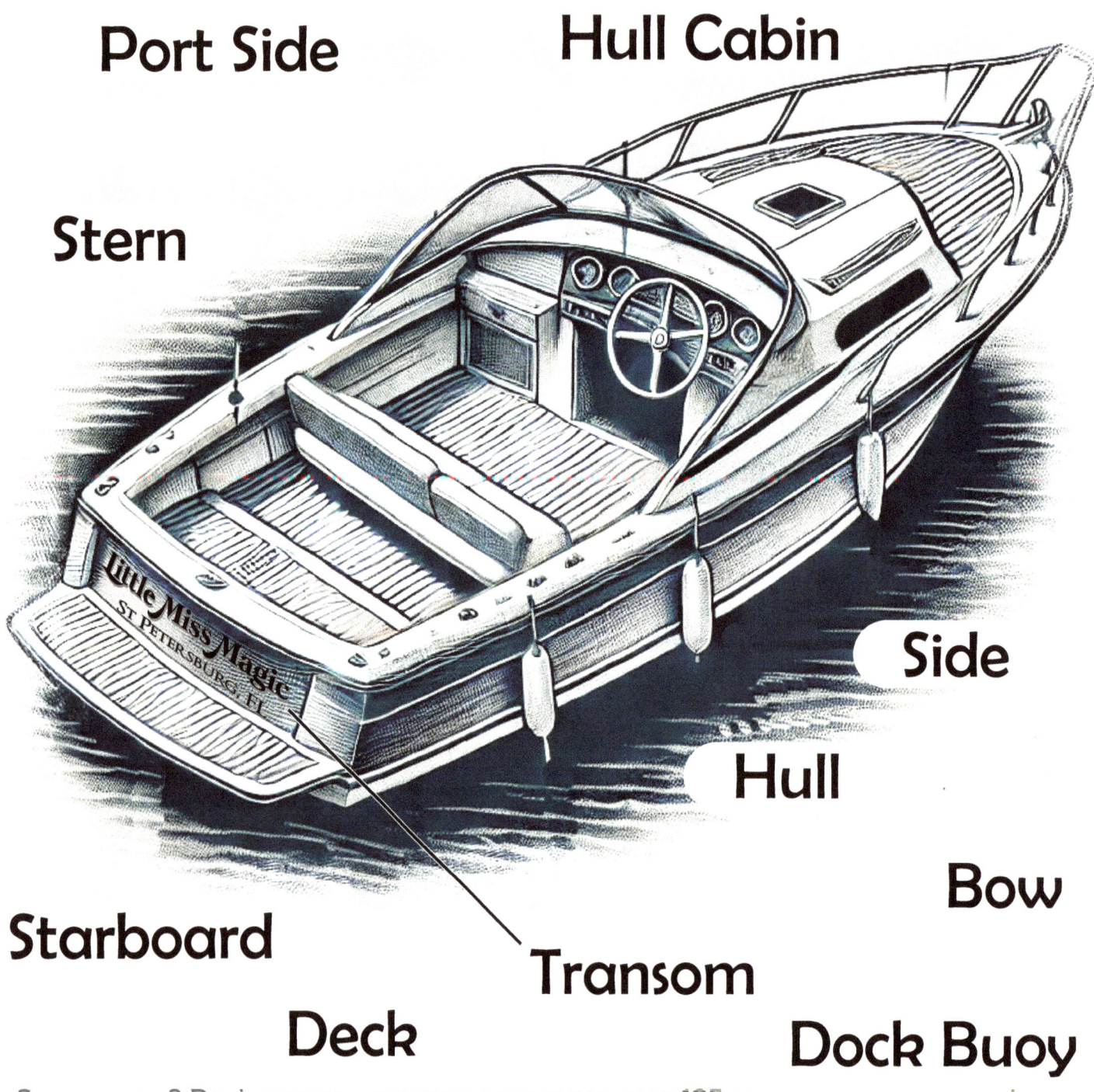

- Port Side
- Hull Cabin
- Stern
- Side
- Hull
- Bow
- Starboard
- Transom
- Deck
- Dock Buoy

STUCK AT SEA? DON'T WORRY — SET YOUR COURSE FOR PAGE 105 TO FIND THE ANSWER KEY!

"If your boat's name doesn't make people smile, you're doing it wrong."
— Unknown"

"You can't buy happiness, but you can buy a boat—and that's pretty close."
— Unknown"

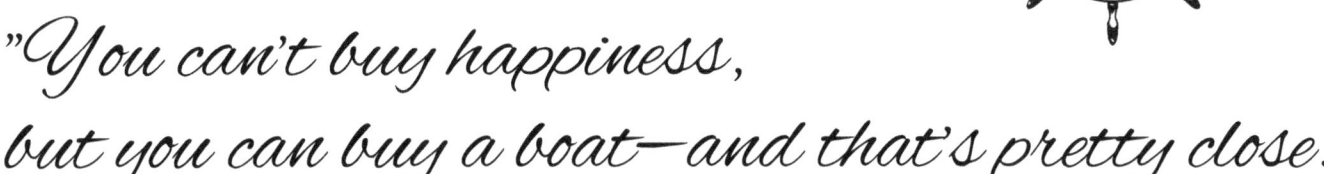

"The only thing more important than your boat's name is your boat's coffee."
— Unknown"

"Boats are like friends; they don't judge, they just float."
—Unknown"

"When in doubt, just name it 'Seas the Day.' It's always a good pun."
— Unknown"

"Woof. I still like 'Sea You Later.'"
— Lucy

Anchor Your Mind & Take a Breather!

Before we dive into the next chapter, take a moment to relax.
Grab some colored pencils, and bring a little life to the sea.
— let your imagination sail. —

Enjoy the break... then we'll jump back into Boat Lettering 101 with fresh eyes!

"Want to share your coloring? Tag @BoatNameGuy on Instagram!"

"Want to share your coloring? Tag @BoatNameGuy on Instagram!"

SERIF: The projections extending off the main strokes of the characters of the serif typefaces. Serifs come in two styles; bracketed and un-bracketed.

STEM: The straight vertical stroke.

COUNTER: The partially or fully enclosed space within a character.

STROKE: A straight or curved line. Other letter parts such as bars, arms, sterns and bowls are collectively referred to as the stroke that makes up a letterform.

BOWL: A curved stroke which creates an enclosed space within a character

BOAT LETTERING 101

CAP HEIGHT
X-HEIGHT
BASELINE

Understanding design, fonts, and what works on water

SHOULDER The curved of the h, m and n.

DESCENDER: The part of the character (g, p, q, y and sometimes j) that descends below the baseline.

by the

"Fonts shown are just a sampling — your name should fit your vibe!"

With over 32,000 font families and over a million fonts that are related, you sure do have your own work cut out for you! You can break this process down by picking a lettering family. For instance Ariel, Comic, Cursive, Script, Impact. And it also depends on the theme of the boat. Beach, Fishing, Sport, Island hopper, bar hopper. Most boat name designers can help you with this and may also have their own fonts that

THE BEST FONT CHOICES 2025

SWING — Boat Name Art Design
TAMPA — Boat Name Art Design
MOUNTAINS — Boat Name Art Design
CHINA — BOAT NAME ART DESIGN
XMAS — Boat Name Art Design
GOFE — Boat Name Art Design
Brillo — Boat Name Art Design
WEAR7 — Boat Name Art Design
BERLIN — Boat Name Art Design
YANK — Boat Name Art Design
HONDER — Boat Name Art Design
WOKE — BOAT NAME ART DESIGN

BIG SKY — Boat Name Art Design
Chancery — Boat Name Art Design
BLOODY — BOAT NAME ART DESIGN
Beer Brew — Boat Name Art Design
Brush — Boat Name Art Design
COLLEGE — BOAT NAME ART DESIGN
Casual — Boat Name Art Design
Fancy — Boat Name Art Design
Harlow — Boat Name Art Design
HONEST — BOAT NAME ART DESIGN
LUCY — Boat Name Art Design
COOKIE — BOAT NAME ART DESIGN

"Playful meets personality."

Lettering Styles

When Choosing the right font for your boat name, start by determining a category of fonts that match the theme you are going for. For instance a party boat would be considered a fancy or script kind of font. A formal or conservative font you would be looking at a Basic

PARTY BOAT

Pieces of Eight

My Boat Name
ABCDEFHJIJK LMNOPQRSTUVWXYZ
A B C D E F G H I J K L M N O P Q R S T U V W X Y Z

Pirates Bay

My Boat Name
ABCDEFHJIJKLMNOPQRSTUVWXYZ
abcdefghijklmnopqrstuvwxyz

Yikes

My Boat Name
ABCDEFHJIJKLMNOPQRSTUVWXYZ
abcdefghijklmnopqrstuvwxyz

SPORTY FISHING

Trajan

My Boat Name
ABCDEFHJIJKLMNOPQRSTUVWXYZ
ABCDEFGHIJKLMNOPQRSTUVWXYZ

Honest John's

My Boat Name
ABCDEFHJIJKLMNOPQRSTUVWXYZ
ABCDEFGHIJKLMNOPQRSTUVWXYZ

Full House

My Boat Name
ABCDEFHJIJKLMNOPQRSTUVWXYZ
ABCDEFGHIJKLMNOPQRSTUVWXYZ

FANCY BOATING

X-mas Day

My Boat Name
ABCDEFHJIJKLMNOPQRSTUVWXYZ
abcdefghijklmnopqrstuvwxyz

Bella Donna

My Boat Name
ABCDEFHJIJKLMNOPQRSTUVWXYZ
abcdefghijklmnopqrstuvwxyz

"Font choice should reflect your boat's energy — bold for sporty, script for elegant, and casual for chill vibes."

FORMAL/ WORLD TRAVELER

Algerian
MY BOAT NAME
ABCDEFHJIJKLMNOPQRSTUVWXYZ

Victorian
My Boat Name
ABCDEFHJIJKLMNOPQRSTUVWXYZ
abcdefghijklmnopqrstuvwxyz

Black Chancery
My Boat Name
ABCDEFHJIJKLMNOPQRSTUVWXYZ
abcdefghijklmnopqrstuvwxyz

ISLAND OR BAR HOPPING

My Boat Name
ABCDEFHJIJKLMNOPQRSTUVWXYZ
abcdefghijklmnopqrstuvwxyz

Venetian

My Boat Name
ABCDEFHJIJKLMNOPQRSTUVWXYZ
abcdefghijklmnopqrstuvwxyz

Harlow Solid

My Boat Name
ABCDEFHJIJKLMNOPQRSTUVWXYZ
abcdefghijklmnopqrstuvwxyz

Harlow Solid

TOP 20 MOST USED BOAT NAME FONTS

DID YOU KNOW THE SENTENCE "THE QUICK BROWN FOX JUMPS OVER THE LAZY DOG" USES EVERY LETTER IN THE ENGLISH ALPHABET?

Brush Script	The Quick Brown Fox Jumps Over The Lazy Dog
Bully	The Quick Brown Fox Jumps Over The Lazy Dog
Cartoon Shout	THE QUICK BROWN FOX JUMPS OVER THE LAZY DOG
Friday Night	THE QUICK BROWN FOX JUMPS OVER THE LAZY DOG
Graffiti Treat	The quick brown fox jumps over the lazy dog
Harlow Solid	The Quick Brown Fox Jumps Over The Lazy Dog
Honest John	THE QUICK BROWN FOX JUMPS OVER THE LAZY DOG
Light Foot	THE QUICK BROWN FOX JUMPS OVER THE LAZY DOG
Marina	The quick brown fox jumps over the lazy dog
Motion Picture	The Quick Brown Fox Jumps Over The Lazy Dog
Optimus Princeps	THE QUICK BROWN FOX JUMPS OVER THE LAZY DOG
Pieces of Eight	THE QUICK BROWN FOX JUMPS OVER THE LAZY DOG
Reporter Two	The quick brown fox jumps over the lazy dog
Sergeant Six Pack	THE QUICK BROWN FOX JUMPS OVER THE LAZY DOG
Tale Of Hawks	The Quick Brown Fox Jumps Over The Lazy Dog
Trajan Pro	THE QUICK BROWN FOX JUMPS OVER THE LAZY DOG
Victorian	The quick brown fox jumps over the lazy dog
Yikes	The quick brown fox jumps over the lazy dog
Bella Donna	The quick brown fox jumps over the lazy dog
Wreckage	THE QUICK BROWN FOX JUMPS OVER THE LAZY DOG

A good place to start off finding a font is at dafont.com.
They have a huge archive of freely downloadable fonts.
Browse by alphabetical listing, by style, by author or by popularity.
You can type in your boat name to see the preview of each style font

Once you break it down to the style font you want, you can contact the Boat Name Guy to see more examples of how your boat name would look on your boat.
"Visit www.BoatNameGuy.com/Boat-Name-Form to test your favorite style."

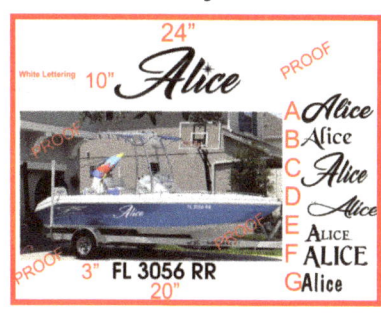

Boat Lettering Fonts Should Relate to Your Boat Name Theme

What Font to use makes or breaks the Boat Name!
It all depends on what your boat name is. If your boat name is "Wet Wind", you probably don't want to see the name in a block letter. But it sure would look good if the word wind was in a whispering font and the Wet word looked like the word was wet in the wind. That is why boat lettering fonts should relate to your boat names theme.

So before I start proofing a boat name, I first go through some fonts that look good. I pick fonts that either looks wet or windy. Latter on I can make changes to each letter if need be. I throw in a couple of plain ones just to help with the visual of the name. Sometimes names get to fancy or are flooded with graphics and the name is hard to see from a distant. Or even as far as the dock.

I did a simple search in google and came across a font website that had the look I was thinking of. The font is called wet dream. With some changes to the font I made it look the way I wanted it. Also notice the opening in the "e".

So this would be the first proof I would send a customer that picked this name. It is sometimes overwhelming to see so many fonts and graphics. You may sometimes feel like you want to see it all. Maybe in the near future we will have motion graphics.

Another boat owner wanted to have the name Aqua Marie. The theme of this particular boat had to be about the owner's daughter and a Disney character.

Every boat name that has been thought of usually comes with the work of picking the right boat lettering. Sometimes a font will scream your boat name and then you just know they were meant to be together. Out of a lineup of ten fonts the boat owner knew that font #1 was the right feel for his marine identity.

Picking the right boat lettering fonts for your boat is crucial. Some believe of just having their name in just a basic traditional font. Then later decide that there boat name had no spark.

When you have a graphic artist create your name it is important to explain exactly what you are looking for. The boat name guys form is a great place to start. Then leave the rest to a creative artist to do the rest.

There are some boat owners that make the mistake of ordering from those websites that the customer designs themselves. But always comes up short with a lack of options to change anything. You are basically stuck using only a few font selections and minimum of graphics.
So if you need some boat lettering done to your boat be sure to have the Boat Name Guy help you!

BOAT NAME DESIGN

By now you should have a good idea what font you will want to use with your boat name. The boat name may be fine laid out straight without any design features or you may want to allibriate a little more to match the theme of your boat. Below are some more steps you can take to enhance your boat name.

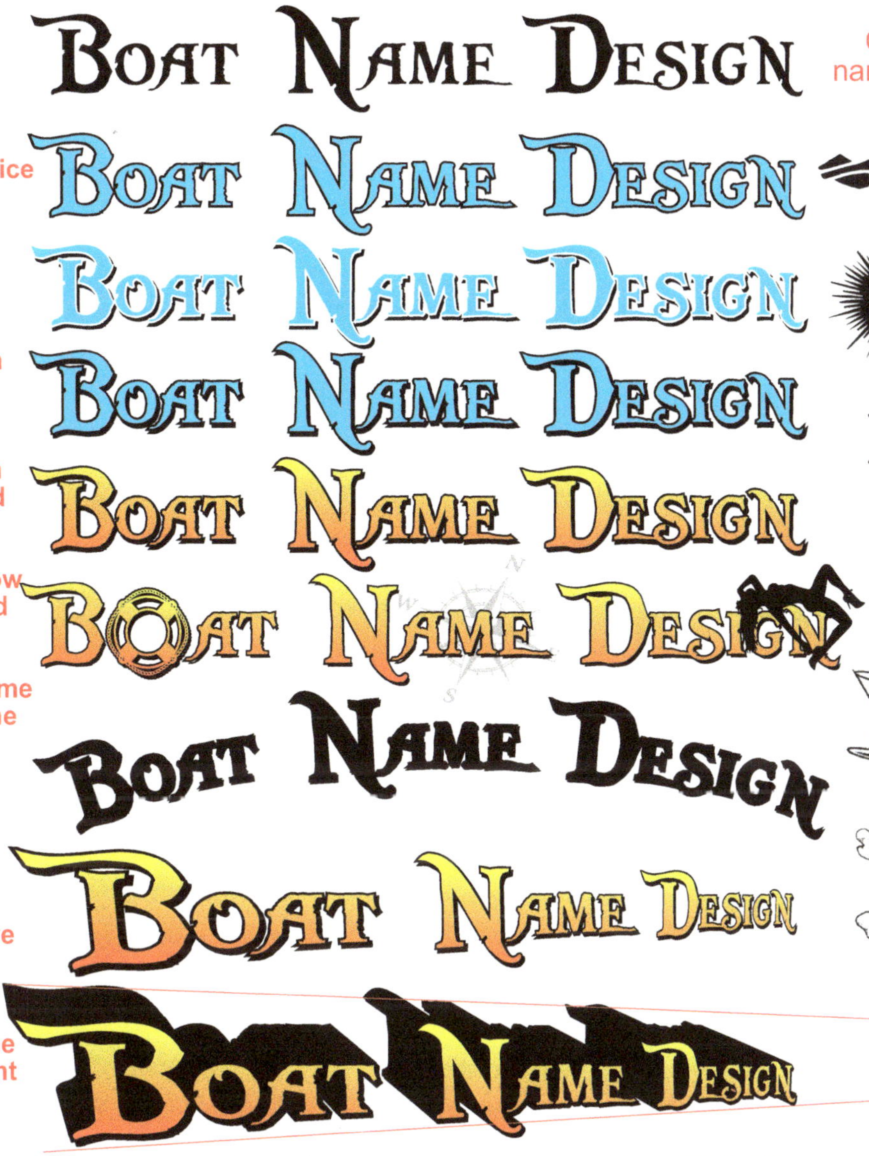

Clip art added to your name to emphasize theme

The font of your choice

Black outline

White outline with cast shadow

Black outline with shadow combined

Fiery Red and Yellow Fountain fill added

Clip art added to name to emphasize theme

Adding curves

Adding Perspective

Extruding the name to a vanishing point

Anything is possible when creating your boat name. Keeping it simple is sometimes the best option.

Photos, clipart and icons can be easily found on a google search. Type in the theme words and click "search images.

"All clip art shown can be customized or swapped to match your theme."

BOAT NAME COLORS

When choosing your favorite colors for your new boat name, keep in mind the colors of the rest of your boat. If your boats Bimini is navy blue and the pin-stripping is grey and black, you may want to go with the same colors so it looks like it came right out of the boat factory.

It makes the name look like it was custom designed specifically for your boat. Picking out complementing colors for your boat can make or break the final design.

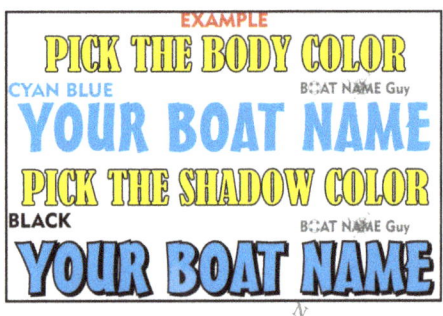

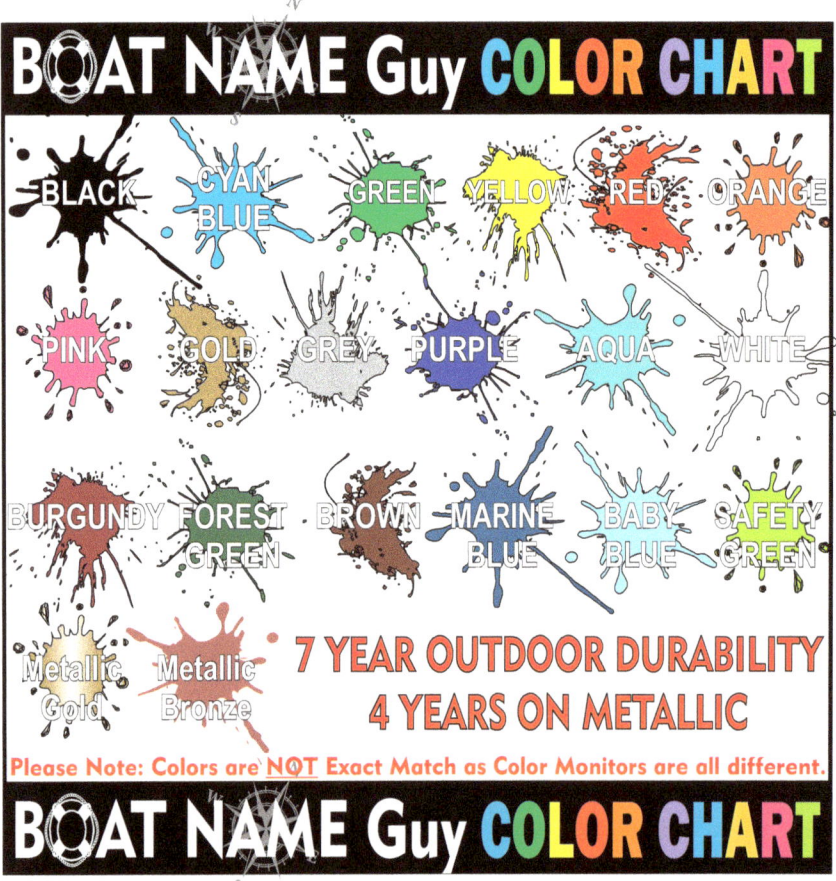

This color chart is being used on Etsy and Ebay to show the colors that are available from the Boat Name Guy.

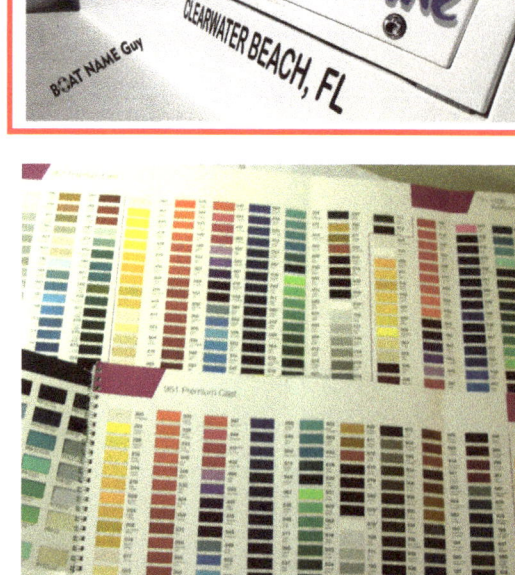

There are hundreds of colors to choose from.

"A good color match can make it look factory-original."

+ ART ACCENT

**IF YOU DON'T SEE WHAT YOU LIKE...
TELL ME IN DESCRIPTION WHAT YOU WANT!**

"The sea may be unpredictable, but your boat's name shouldn't be."
– Unknown

MEASUREMENTS

Now that you have a good photograph to work with it is time to measure her up. Knowing where all the door jams, drain holes and hatch handles are will help in the designing process.

The sizes below on a Maritimo 59 shows the precise measurements of the door and side panels. Also note the door hinges that are 14" in height. So it is safe to say that the lettering can be 13" height x 90" width. The graph behind the lettering can be 27" height x 16" width.

As you can also see that the lettering landed in the middle and without hitting the door jams besides the "T" in Southern. A little extra installation time is required when working around obstacles like this. Making sure that the graphics get cut correctly to fold in the cracks of the door jams.

There was plenty of room for the port name on this boat. We had 6" height by 32" + in width. So it was safe to make the port name 4" H x 32" W, in that area.

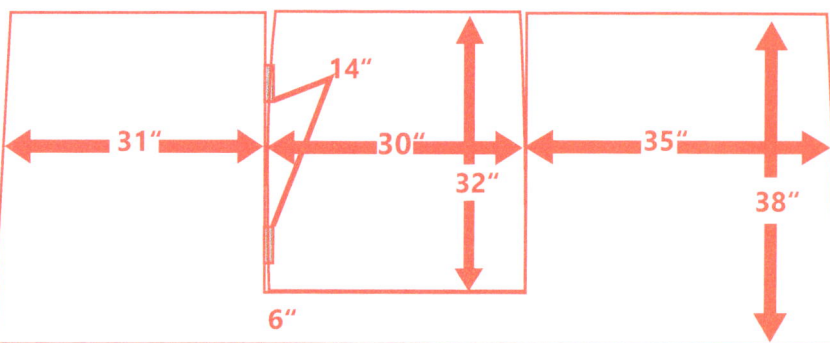

FINISHED PRODUCT

MEASURE TWICE PRINT ONCE

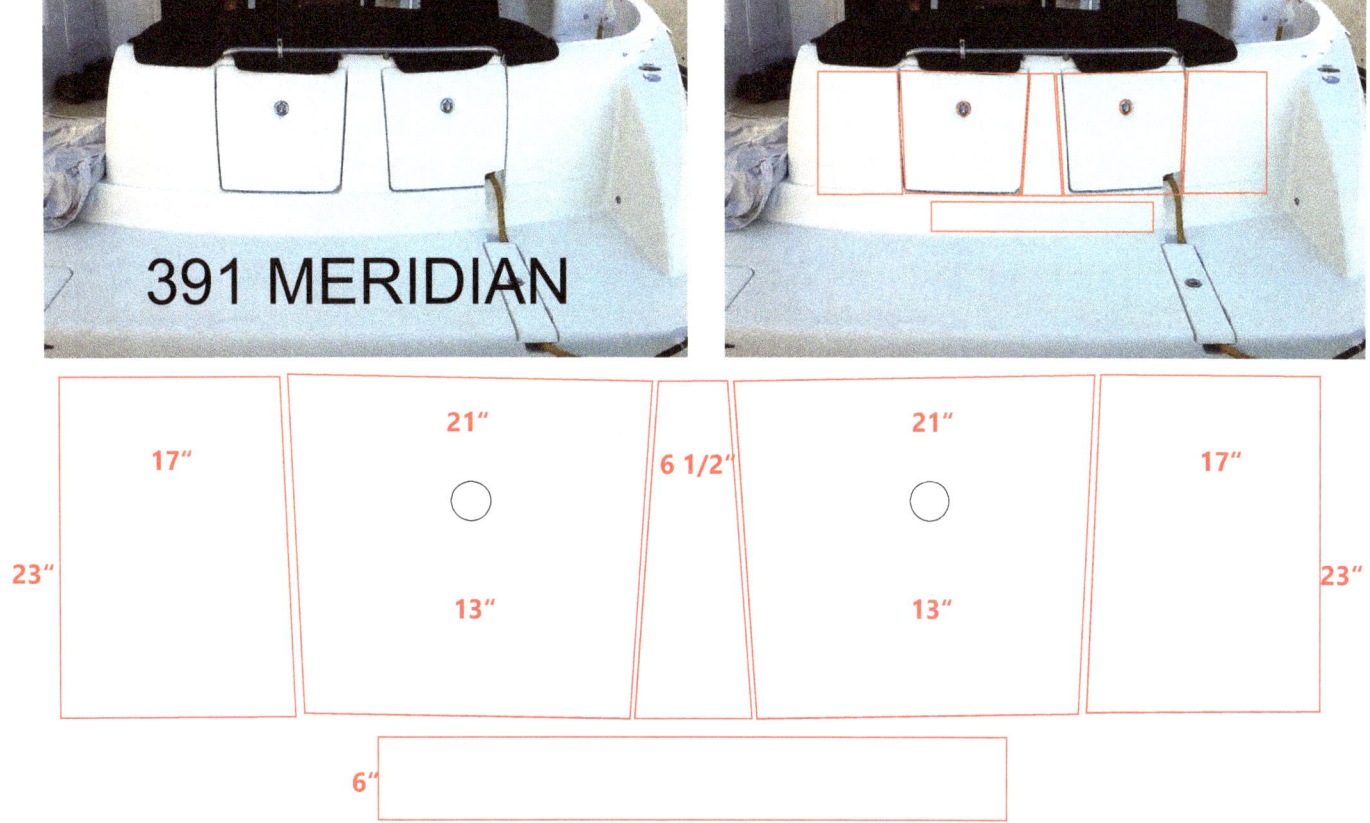

"Fit your design to the boat — not the other way around."

Before you hit "print," take a breath — and take a measurement.
Then take one more.

Getting your boat name sized right is just as important as picking the perfect font.
You want to make sure your name fits the space, has enough breathing room,
and is easy to read from a distance.
Whether it's going on the transom, hull, or cabin, don't guess. Tape out the space, step back, and visualize i

Measure twice — so you only have to print once.

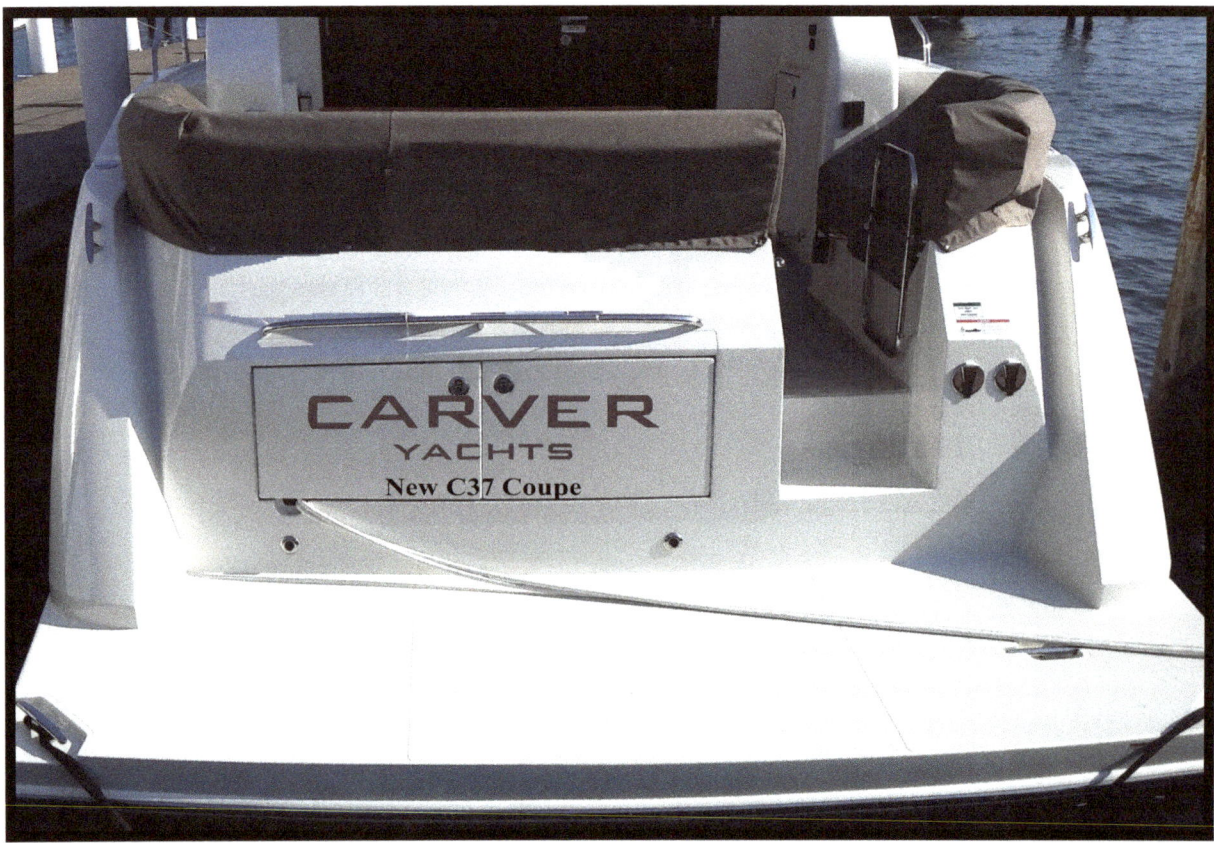

"Final Touches: Real Installs, Real Results"

Mermaid's Treasure
Set Sail on a Word Search Adventure!

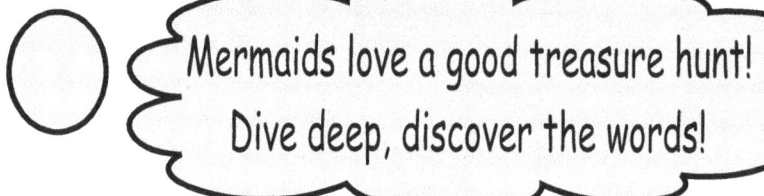

Mermaids love a good treasure hunt! Dive deep, discover the words!

Captain Deck Dock Marina Mermaid Nautical Ocean Port Sailboat
Skipper Starboard Tiki Transom Trawler Waves Yacht

```
S J M A R I N A C L Y
A X D R A O B R A T S
I N R Y A C H T Z M Y
L I E K S I K I T O I
B A P C Z E T E N S R
O T P O D R V A X N E
A P I D O E E A V A L
T A K P C C C A W R W
V C S Q O E S K B T A
F G D I A M R E M O R
N A U T I C A L M K T
```

STUCK AT SEA? DON'T WORRY—SET YOUR COURSE FOR PAGE 105 TO FIND THE ANSWER KEY!

"A bad day on the boat still beats a good day at the office!"
– Unknown"

"Sail away from the safe harbor, but don't forget the name tag." – Unknown

What Is a Hailing Port?

"It's more than a location—it's part of your boat's story."

If your boat is U.S. Coast Guard documented, you are required to display:
- Your boat's name
- A hailing port (City and State)

Both must appear together on the exterior hull.

You may choose any U.S. city and state for your hailing port when filing your CG-1258 documentation form. It does not have to be the city where your boat is physically located.

Your hailing port must be displayed in letters at least four inches high, just like the boat name.

Try saying your top name ideas out loud to a friend or on the dock!

Pro Tip:

Even if you're not required to display a hailing port, it's a great design opportunity.

Choose a port name that complements your boat's story,
and match the font style to your boat name for a cohesive look.
Whether it's serious or silly, a well-placed port name adds polish and personality.

What If Your Boat Is Not Documented?

If your vessel is not documented, you can still display a hailing port — and many boaters do!

It adds personality, makes your boat stand out at the marina, and starts conversations. Some owners choose:
- Their hometown or dream port
- A playful or fictional place ("Rum Cay" or "No Worries, FL")
- The city where they fell in love with boating

Whether it's legal, local, or just for laughs — your port name tells part of your story.

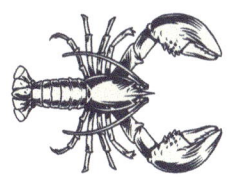

You are not required to display a hailing port (City and State) unless the boat is U.S. Coast Guard documented.
All documented vessels in the United States are required to display a name and hailing port on the hull.

You may select any U.S. City and State as the hailing port on the CG-1258 Application for Documentation if this is your intention.
Also your port name needs to be at least four inches in height.
If your boat is not a documented boat then you can put anything you like on there. And still would be a good idea and conversation starter.

BOAT NAME PROOF

"Design approval happens here before anything is cut or printed."

This is where it all begins — the digital proof created in CorelDRAW.
Every boat name starts with a custom design laid out for the customer to preview.
This proof shows how the name will look on the actual boat, often with size references, font choices, and sample placements.
I'll usually send this to the customer for approval before anything is cut or printed, and it gives them a chance to request changes or additions.
The proof includes colors, layout, and often optional shading or outlines.

VECTOR LINES (Cut Path Preparation)

Once the layout is approved, I prepare the design for production.
This image shows the vector outlines — the paths the cutter or printer will follow. You'll see tight, clean lines that make up the final shapes. Every curve and edge matters here. This is what ensures the graphics are sharp and perfectly aligned during installation.
If it's a plotted vinyl job, this is the exact cut path.
If it's printed, the lines are used to contour-cut the full-color print cleanly.

FINAL INSTALLATION (On the Boat)

Here's the finished result installed directly onto the boat. The name has been applied using high-
quality vinyl or full-color print depending on the job.
You can see how the original digital design comes to life on the hull.
The size, spacing, and layout all match the proof — and everything was positioned using measurements taken during the design stage.
From concept to completion, this final step is where it all comes together.

Some boat name lettering and graphics are requested to be in a full color. In other words you can see the fade of each color compared to just solid spot colors. It can be considered that three to four colors on a boat name logo could be declared as a full color if that's all the color that is needed in your logo.

4 Color Boat Name   FULL Color Boat Name

PLOTTED PRINTED

A four colored boat name like Sandy's beach above was plotted out in separate colors. Then each color is installed on the boat separately until the boat name logo is achieved.

The technology for printing boat names has come a long way and today we are able to make full Color Prints last for years. The process is still done on vinyl. Large format printing machines can print on a white 3M vinyl. After printing the graphics, another large laminating machine laminates on top of it to help protect from scratches and UV rays.

Here are some of the pros and cons of having a full-color graphic rather than having solid base vinyl colors.

- Still to this day solid non printed vinyl colors will not fade as fast as a printed vinyl.
- Full color printed graphics are a little more costly to design and create out of 3m material.
- The full color boat name is clearly more vivid and pleasing to the eye.
- It is important to have someone design it correctly to compliment your boat and to stay away from high contrasted that could make the boat logo muddy and not visible from a distance.
- If part of a full color graphic some how gets damaged it is a bit more costly to repair.

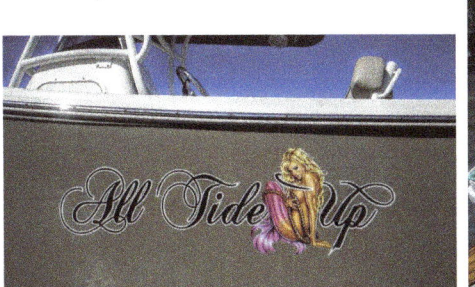

Nautical Know-How!

Time to drop anchor and have some fun—take a break from all that boat naming history!

Across

1. - "The flat part at the back of the boat—perfect for a name!"

3. - "The boss of the boat, also known as the skipper!"

4. - "The water says hello by doing this in the ocean."

6. - "Helps you find your way when you're lost at sea."

8. - "The right side of a boat when you're looking ahead."

10. - "Where boats rest when they're not sailing."

12. - "What the captain uses to steer the ship."

14. - "The place where the sky meets the water—so dreamy!"

15. - "A long journey across the sea."

Down

2. - "Someone who works or travels on a boat."

5. - "What keeps the boat from floating away? (Hint: It's heavy!)"

7. - "The left side of a boat when you're facing forward."

9. - "A floating marker in the water—sometimes it even lights up!"

11. - "The backbone of the boat, running along the bottom."

13. - "Another word for a sailor or seafarer."

STUCK AT SEA? DON'T WORRY—SET YOUR COURSE FOR PAGE 105 TO FIND THE ANSWER KEY!

Is It Really Bad Luck to Change a Boat Name?

There's always that moment of hesitation…
You're standing there, scraper in hand, wondering—
"Will the boat forgive me?"
Maybe the name has been lucky. Maybe it's part of the boat's soul.

Nautical tradition says changing a boat's name is bad luck—unless it's done properly. But don't worry, there are a few clever (and fun) ways to calm the boating gods and give your vessel a fresh start:

• **Hide the Original Name**
   Keep the old name alive—but hidden. Reprint it in a tiny font and place it under the bow or somewhere out of sight. You'll know it's there, and so will the boat.

• **Sage & Spirit Cleanse**
   Give your boat a clean slate—literally and spiritually. Burn sage onboard to "clear the old energy." Metaphysical shops often offer guidance and kits to help you do it right.

• **Host a Renaming Ceremony**
   This can be as serious or as silly as you like. Some invite a priest, some a pirate. Champagne (for the boat *and* the crew) is a must. The tradition says you must first strike the old name from Neptune's Ledger before offering the new one.

Remember: traditions exist for fun, respect, and storytelling. Do what feels right for you. If you take the time to honor the process—even with humor—the boat will probably understand.

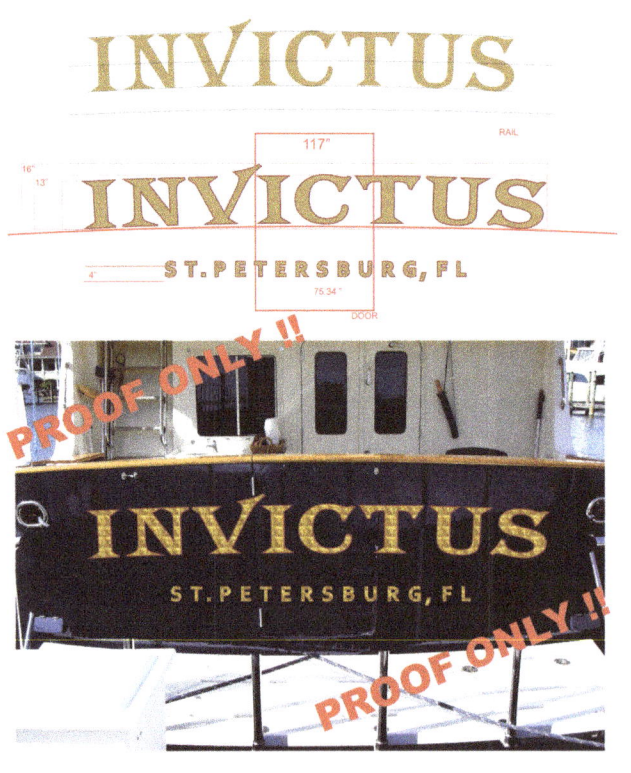

How to Remove A Boat Name
"Step-by-step guide for a clean start."

Removing an old boat name—especially one that's been on for 10+ years—can be tricky. The vinyl acts like a sunblock, preserving the shiny gelcoat underneath while the rest of the boat weathers and fades. That's why you'll often see a "ghost" of the old name even after it's removed.

Here's a safe, effective way to remove it:

1. **Heat and Peel Carefully**
   Use a heat gun and a plastic razor scraper. Heat small sections just enough to soften the vinyl—don't overdo it or you'll risk damaging the gelcoat.

2. **Remove the Adhesive**
   After peeling the vinyl, use a rag and some Goof Off or acetone to wipe away the sticky residue. Keep turning the rag so you're not rubbing the glue back on.

3. **Scrape Gently as Needed**
   Use a plastic scraper at a low angle (around 40° or less) to help lift stubborn spots without gouging the surface.

4. **Tackle the Ghosting**
   If you can still see the outline of the name ("ghosting"), lightly wet sand the area using fine-grit sandpaper (like 1500–2000 grit) with water. Only sand over the ghosted areas.

5. **Polish and Protect**
   Finish with a rubbing compound or cleaner wax to even out the surface and restore shine. Several coats may be needed. Some ghosting may still be visible in certain lighting, depending on how long the name was on and your local climate.

BOAT NAME REMOVAL

56"
14"
4"
Midnight Lady
ST. PETERSBURG, FL

A Midnight Lady
B Midnight Lady
C Midnight Lady
D Midnight Lady
E Midnight Lady
F MIDNIGHT LADY
G MIDNIGHT LADY
H Midnight Lady
I Midnight Lady
J Midnight Lady
K Midnight Lady
L Midnight Lady
M Midnight Lady
N Midnight Lady

#BoatNameGuy

SEA BLUE LETTERING   Blue Glow Drop Shadow

PROOF

 **DETAILED**

 **INSTALLING**

"From removal to reveal a full transformation!"

FINISHED PRODUCT

NAMING & RENAMING RITUALS

Naming a boat is a tradition that dates back thousands of years — and doing it *right* is said to keep you in Neptune's good graces. If you're renaming a vessel, many sailors believe it's important to first **"de-name"** it to avoid bad luck. Once the old name is respectfully erased from the sea's memory, you're clear to bless your boat with her new identity.

Ceremonies can be as simple or elaborate as you like. Whether it's just you and your dog at the dock or a full party with friends, it's the intention that counts. And yes — it almost always includes **a little bubbly** over the bow.

Boat Naming Ceremony Checklist:

- ○ Remove all traces of the old name (vinyl letters, keychains, etc.)
- ○ Speak a de-naming ritual (can be serious or funny)
- ○ Prepare your new boat name reveal
- ○ Write or print a boat blessing (see sample prayer below)
- ○ Bring champagne (one bottle for the boat, one for the crew)
- ○ Invite witnesses (optional, but fun)
- ○ Pour or toss champagne over the bow (never drink first!)
- ○ Toast to fair winds and safe voyages
- ○ Record the moment — photos or logbook entry

PRO TIP:
Write your own blessing using your boat's personality. Funny, heartfelt, or poetic — there's no wrong way to do it as long as it's sincere.

PRO TIP:
If your first mate is a dog, let them touch a paw or nose to the hull during the blessing. It's good luck. (And adorable.)

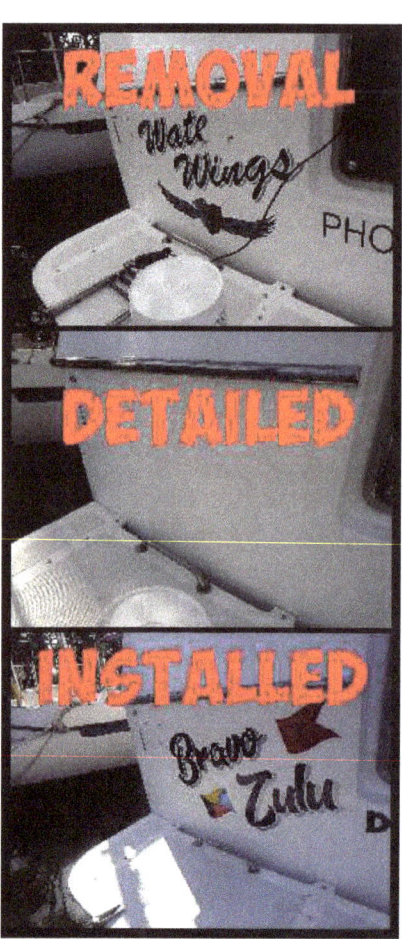

BOAT NAME REMOVAL

BEFORE   **AFTER**

PRO TIP:
Don't just remove the name — erase the *energy*. Some sailors burn the old name written on paper and toss the ashes into the sea (or a firepit if you're docked).

Sample Blessing-Prayer

Oh mighty Neptune, ruler of seas and protector of sailors,
we ask you to forget the former name of this vessel
and accept this new name with favor.

We dedicate this boat, [Insert Boat Name],
to safe journeys, calm waters, and joyful adventures.
Bless all who sail aboard her.
Let the wind be always at our back, and may she return to shore
strong, proud, and true.

BEFORE   **AFTER**

Page 51

DIY INSTALLATION

Take your time and read all the instructions before you begin. It is also recommended that you watch at least two different videos on how to install graphics on Youtube. After watching and reading these instructions you should have a better grasp of what is in tailed.

When you receive your boat name graphics you will see that the vinyl that will be placed on your boat is in between a paper layer of application Tape and a waxed backing. As soon as you receive your graphics, remove them from the box and place them on a flat surface for a few hours.

Make sure where lettering will be applied is thoroughly cleaned of all grease, dirt and wax using glass cleaner. For some stubborn marks, stains and grit try using some Acetone.

Temperature for applying graphics must be between 45 F an 90 F with low humidity.

Paper Towels   Ruler   Squeegee   Painters Tape   Scissors   Exacto Knife   Spray Bottle   Razor

Tools you will need.. Ruler, Squeegee, Painters Tape, Scissors, Spray bottle filled with a mixture of dish soap and water. (The mixture ratio is; 2 drops of soap to 1 cup of water) Paper towels, Razor blade to remove any grit away from boat.

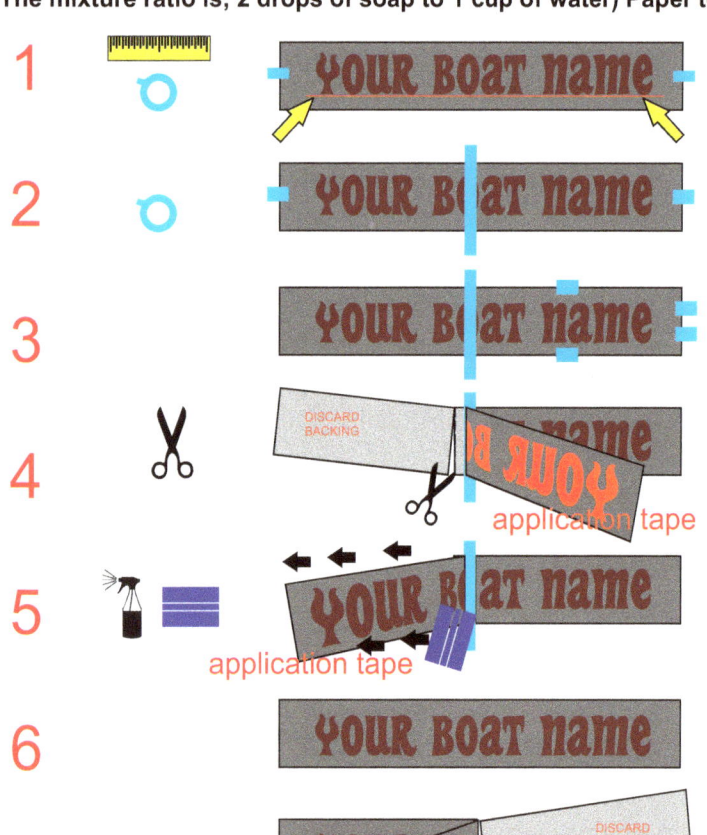

1. Place masking tape to the edges of the graphic. Then place the graphic where you think you would like it. Measure the graphic using the bottom of the letters as a guide.

2. When you decide you like the boat name in its location then mask off the graphic in the middle and all edges. Take a step back to make sure it looks good.

3. Pull the masking tape away from the graphic leaving tape only in the middle and and right side.

4. Continue to remove the backing of the graphic from the lettering and transfer paper. Making sure all the graphic in only on the application tape!

5. Discard the backing paper and then pull the application tape on to the boat keeping it taunt and squeegeing it outward. Burnishing the lettering on to the boat. Lightly spray a small amount of your solution.

6. Now that the left side of the graphic is on the boat, remove all of the masking tape.

7. Pull the rest of the application tape away from the backing and discard. (As in step 4)

8. Squeegee the graphic on to the boat as in step 5. Again using a small amount of your solution.

9. Continue to squeegee all of the graphic in all directions making sure all bubbles are out and away. Here you can spray the whole graphic.

10. Now remove the application tape by pulling down and away on top of its self slowly. Do not pull at a 90 degree angle. Use the exacto knife to pop any bubbles that may still exist.

The Tools of the trade

WATCH A PROFESSIONAL INSTALL A BOAT NAME

MOBILE SERVICES

WE COME TO YOU !

Installing a boat name is a craft of its own.

It often means working in tight, uncomfortable spots—bending, stretching, and sweating for that perfect placement.
Every inch counts, so careful measuring is key to a great result.
Like the saying goes: *Measure twice, install once.*
This guide walks you through the steps, but your patience and precision make all the difference.
Take your time, and let the process be part of the pride.

"Seeing is believing. That's My Girl went from concept to completion flawlessly."

ANCHORS AWAY WITH WORD SCRAMBLES!

1. Take the scrambled word and try to rearrange the letters to form a boat-related word.
2. **Match the letters**: Once you've figured out the word, write it down on the line under the scrambled.
3. **Check it twice**: After completing the puzzle, see if all your answers match the answers below!

Have fun, and may your boat journey be smooth and victorious!

1. TBAO
___

2. LSIA
___

3. RATEIP
___

4. KHOO
___

5. VEAW
___

6. FART
___

7. HRON
___

8. TYJET
___

9. NACNON
___

10. OTORM
___

11. TRENS
___

12. MACPSOS
___

13. HIFS
___

14. HAYCT
___

15. ETID
___

16. ELGED
___

17. TNSRE
___

18. RANIMA
___

19. NIF
___

20. NELI
___

STUCK AT SEA? DON'T WORRY — SET YOUR COURSE FOR PAGE 87 TO FIND THE ANSWER KEY!

Registration Numbers

I know what you're thinking. You want a registration number to match your boat name like on the back of the transom! Or numbers that look like a Salt Life font.

Well it is a free world out there, so if you want to see your States registration numbers in a whisperer font with skull bones, have at it!

Know The Law

If your vessel requires registration, it is illegal to operate it or allow others to operate your vessel unless it is registered and numbered as described above.

Just know the rules before you go out to sea. And when I say rules I mean Your states boating laws. Every state is different, so make sure you go to your states government page and check.

In Florida it states in Ch. 327 and Ch. 328 , Florida Statutes. Also found at
http://myfwc.com/boating/regulations/

The Registration number must be in the front part of the bow above the waterline. Letters must be a block Ariel font and at least 3" in height. The color should be in contrast of the hull

When you register your boat you will also need to put a validation decal on the port (Left) side of the vessel when using Florida waters. The Decal needs to be within 6" of either before or after the registration numbers. I like to put them before the numbers on the star board side and after on the port side. You have up to 30 days from purchase of the vessel to do this.

Letters must be separated from the numbers by a hyphen or space equal to letter width.
For Example: FL 5678 GR or FL-5678-GR

Of course you must have your Certificate of Registration on board with all your other important documentation. This should be available for inspection by an enforcement officer whenever the boat is in operation. You should keep all your credentials preferably in dry storage.

Now with that being said do you think it would be okay to have your registration number any other way? Sure! We just need to be a little creative... We could do it in two colors and make the bold font a little fancy like this.

Orange with Marine Blue Outline

"These measurements refer to minimum height requirements for legal compliance. Double-check with your state."

Some insist on having the registration number designed radical and in theme of their boat.

Please note that an enforcement officer may over look this small crime. If at all they may just give you a warning. It is your call to wonder how many times you will come across law enforcement out on your journeys.

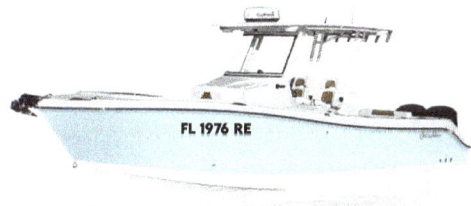

Other Things you should know

A Certificate of Title proves ownership. All vessels are required to have a Certificate of Title. The only exceptions are:
- A non-motorized vessel less than 16 feet in length
- A vessel used exclusively on private lakes and ponds
- Vessels documented with the U.S. Coast Guard

The owner of a registered vessel must notify the county tax collector within 30 days if he or she changes address.

The owner of a registered vessel must notify the Florida Department of Highway Safety and Motor Vehicles within 30 days if the vessel is sold, stolen, destroyed, abandoned, or lost.

Vessels must be registered and numbered within 30 days of purchase.
If your vessel has a current and valid registration or certificate of number from another U.S. state or territory, you may operate it in Florida for 90 days before you are required to register it in Florida.

Larger recreational vessels, owned by U.S. citizens, may (at the option of the owner) be documented by the U.S. Coast Guard. Call the USCG at 1-800-799-8362 for more information. Documented vessels operating on Florida waters must have a current vessel registration from either Florida or another state.

ORDER YOURS THROUGH ETSY

ALL ORDERS RECEIVE PROOF TO BE APPROVED.

REGISTRATION COLORS AND FONTS

ARIAL FONT RECOMENDED

BLACK	FL 8675 GR
SILVER	FL 8675 GR
ROYAL BLUE	FL 8675 GR
MARINE BLUE	FL 8675 GR
LIGHT BLUE	FL 8675 GR
GREEN	FL 8675 GR
GOLD	FL 8675 GR
FOAM GREEN	FL 8675 GR
MERLOT	FL 8675 GR
RED	FL 8675 GR

OTHER COLORS AVAILABLE

OTHER FONT OPTIONS

ARIAL ROUNDED	FL 8675 GR
AVENIR	FL 8675 GR
DOM BOLD	FL 8675 GR
BULLY	FL 8675 GR
ART BRUSH	FL 8675 GR
COLLEGE SLAB	FL 8675 GR
BIONDI	FL 8675 GR
CARTOON	FL 8675 GR
TWO COLOR OPTION	FL 8675 GR

www.BoatNameGuy.com

READY TO ORDER YOUR NEW NUMBERS
Custom Colors to Match Your Boat

PROOF 3" **FL 1175 SU** 21" X2

#BoatNameGuy — AQUA LETTERS — SILVER CAST SHADOW

REGISTRATION NUMBERS

Boat Name Guy — FAST

Port Names & Hailing Ports

~Required for some, meaningful for all.

If your boat is documented with the U.S. Coast Guard, you're required to display both a boat name and a hailing port on the exterior of the hull—typically centered on the stern (rear) of the vessel. The hailing port must include a city and state, and both the name and port must be in letters at least 4 inches high, clearly visible and easy to read.

Modern boat designs can make this tricky. Transoms are getting sleeker, swim platforms are larger, and there's not always room for a long city name. In tight spaces, it's smart to choose a shorter location name (like "Tampa, FL" instead of "St. Petersburg, Florida") that still meets the requirements.

Even if your boat isn't documented, many owners still proudly display a hailing port. It could be your favorite marina, your hometown, or just a destination that feels like home. Either way, it adds a personal touch and tells the world where your boating story begins.

USCG Quick Compliance Tip:
- Hailing port must include a city and state
- Minimum 4-inch high letters
- Must be legible and durable
- Display on the exterior hull of the stern

Why Port Names Matter

A port name does more than meet Coast Guard rules—it anchors your boat's identity. It tells a story. For some boaters, it's a proud shout-out to their hometown or a tribute to the harbor where their adventures began. For others, it's a dream destination—a sunny place they cruise to every chance they get. Port names can spark conversation, help fellow boaters remember you, and create a sense of belonging no matter where you dock.

BOAT PREFIX ETIQUETTE

Ever see "SS" or "SV" before a boat name and wonder what it means?
These prefixes aren't part of the name — they're shorthand for the **type or purpose** of the boat.

Here are a few of the most common:

- ⚓ **SS** – Steam Ship (used historically for steam-powered ships)
- ⚓ **MV** – Motor Vessel (engine-powered)
- ⚓ **SV** – Sailing Vessel (wind-powered)
- ⚓ **MY** – Motor Yacht
- ⚓ **FV** – Fishing Vessel
- ⚓ **TB** – Tug Boat
- ⚓ **RMS** – Royal Mail Ship (historical mail delivery ships)
- ⚓ **TT** – Tender To (typically a dinghy or small boat used to reach the main vessel)

Should you use one?

☑ Only if you want to. It's not required for recreational boats, but it can add character or clarity—especially on documentation paperwork, signage, or when you want to sound salty at the marina bar.

Example:
SV Seawind or **MY Lucky Lucy**

If you're not sure, just skip it. You don't have to be formal unless you want to sound fancy.

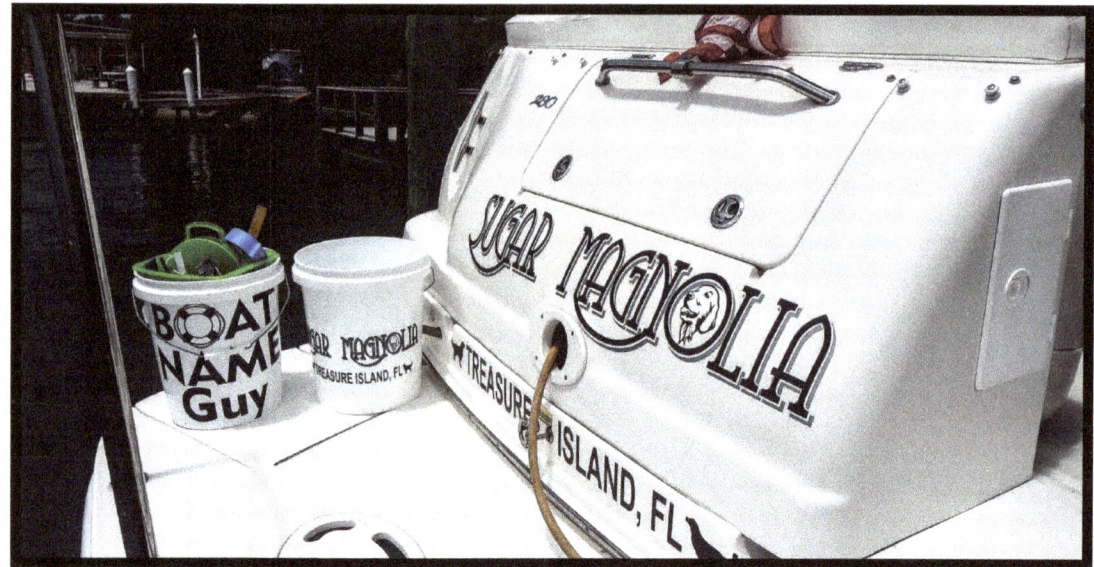

"Bring Your Pup, Don't Leave Them Behind!"
Why leave your best friend at home all alone,
When the sea calls out in a joyful tone?
The sun is shining, the breeze is right,
A perfect day for a dog's delight!
Their tail will wag with the salty air,
Their paws will dance without a care.
The boat is rocking, the waves are free,
A pup on board is the way it should be!
They'll stand at the bow, ears in the wind,
Watching the dolphins, grinning like them.
No lonely sighs, no longing eyes,
Just golden days and ocean skies.
So grab their leash, their favorite toy,
A life vest too—bring the joy!
A captain's best mate has four little paws,
And loves the sea with zero flaws.
Don't leave them home, don't make them wait,
A dog on a boat makes the trip truly great! ⚓

Pro Tip: Add your dog's name to your boat design!
A paw print, silhouette, or playful font can make it even more personal.

NOTES & DOODLES

Pro Tip:

Thought of the perfect boat name?
Try it in *thesaurus.com*
you might discover an even cooler word
you hadn't considered!

_____
_____
_____
_____
_____
_____
_____
_____
_____
_____
_____
_____
_____
_____

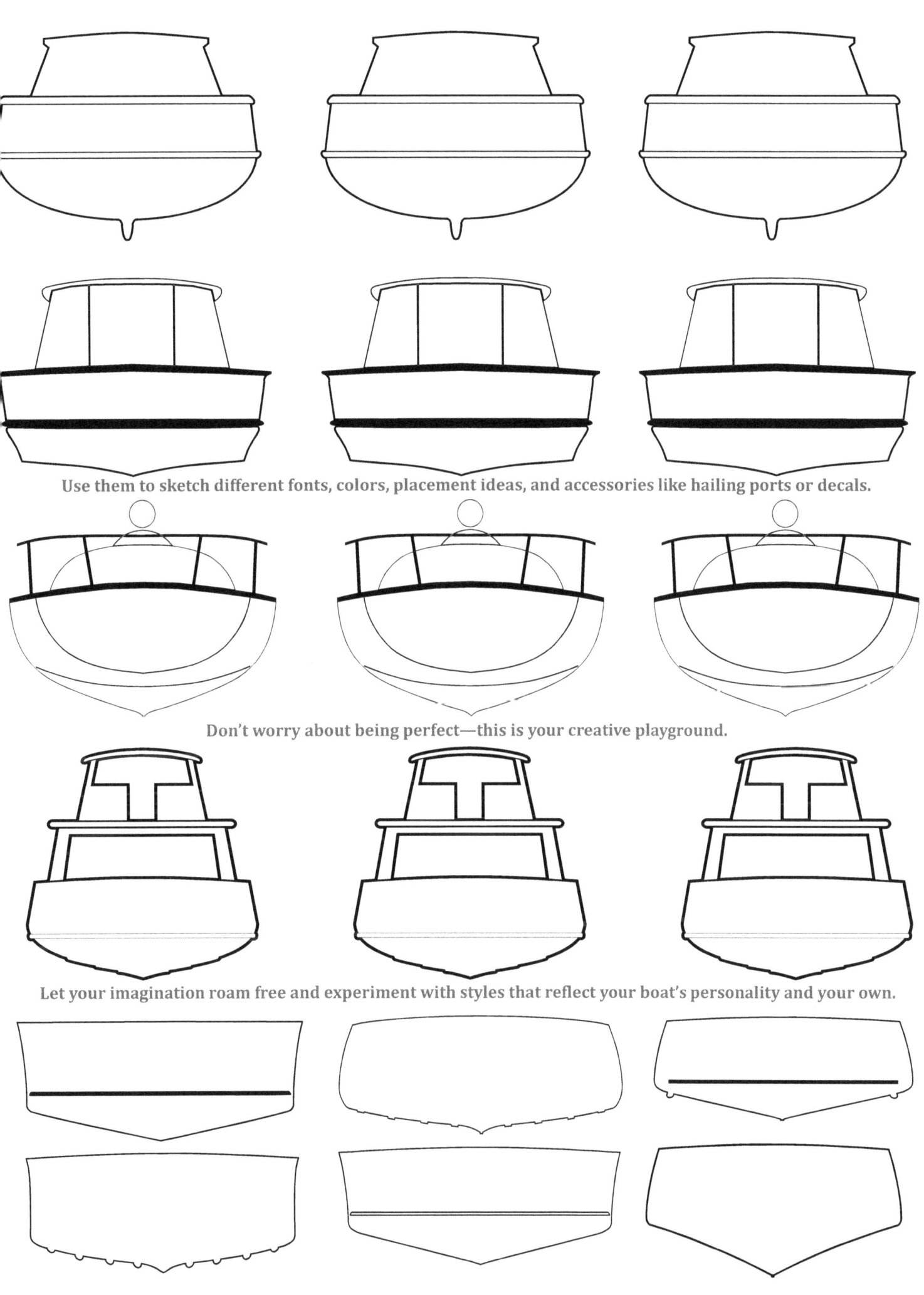

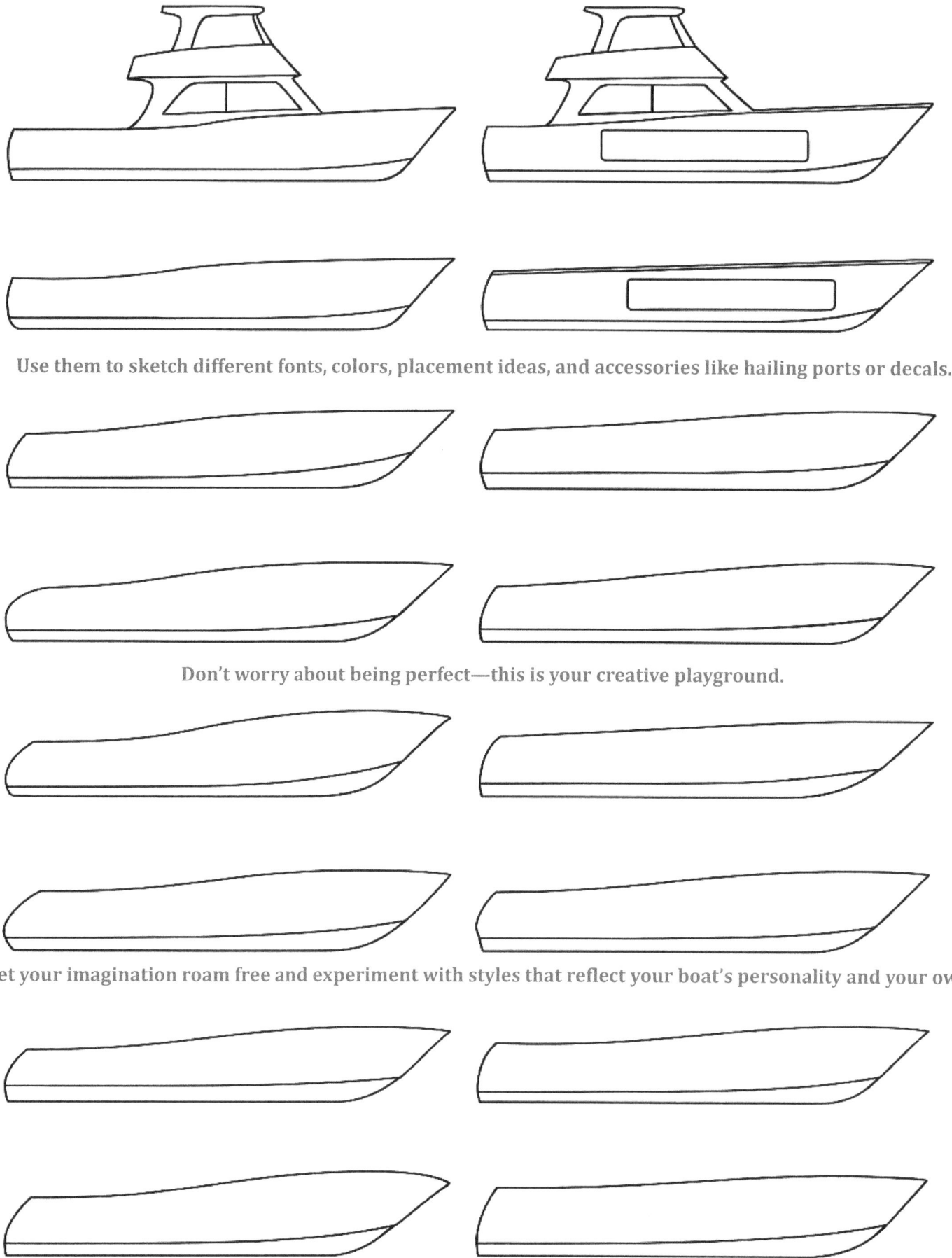

Use them to sketch different fonts, colors, placement ideas, and accessories like hailing ports or decals.

Don't worry about being perfect—this is your creative playground.

Let your imagination roam free and experiment with styles that reflect your boat's personality and your ow

NOTES & DOODLES

Thought of the perfect boat name?
Try it in *thesaurus.com*
you might discover an even cooler word
you hadn't considered!

_____
_____
_____
_____
_____
_____
_____
_____
_____
_____
_____
_____

NOTES & DOODLES

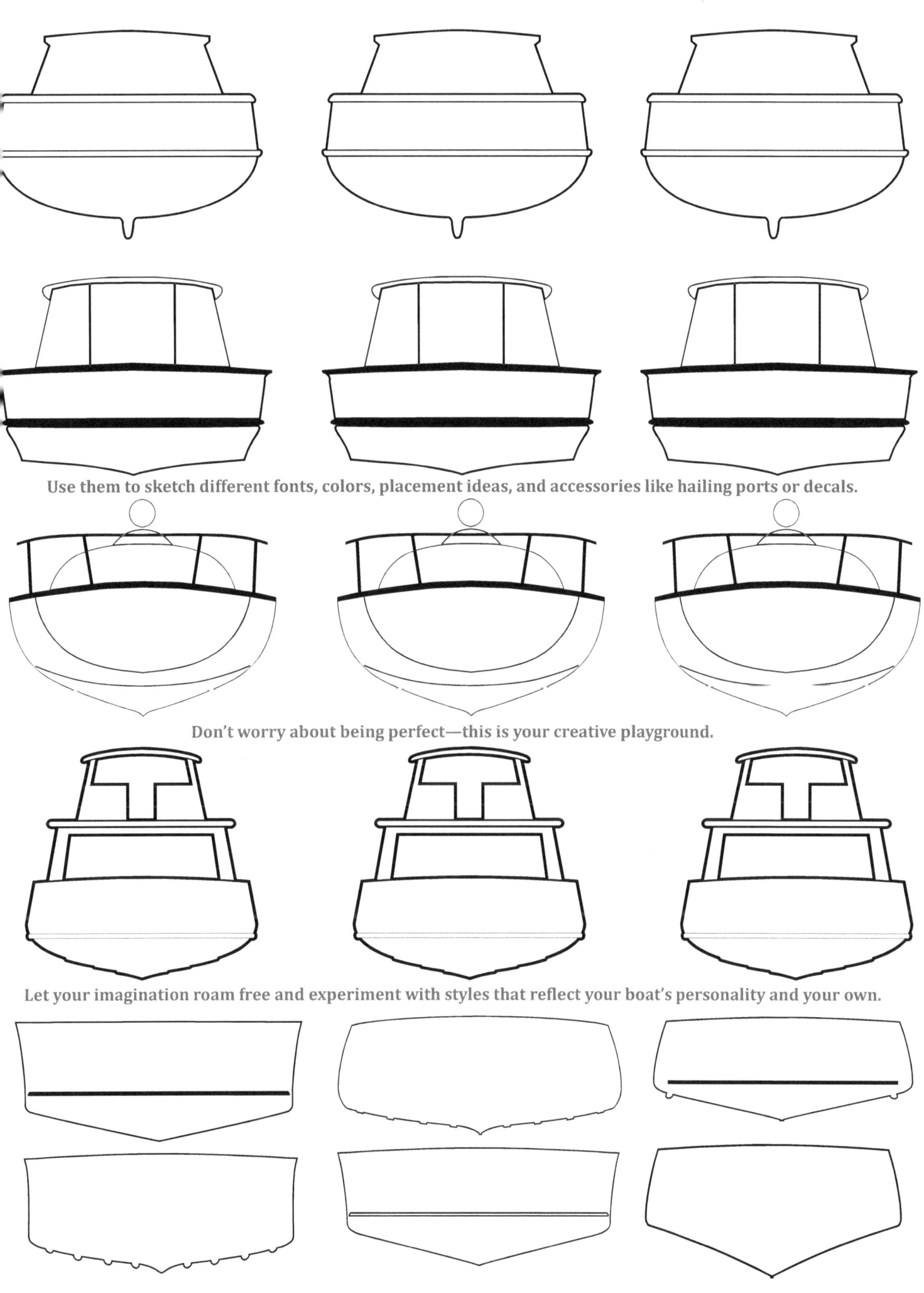

Design Your Dream Name Placement

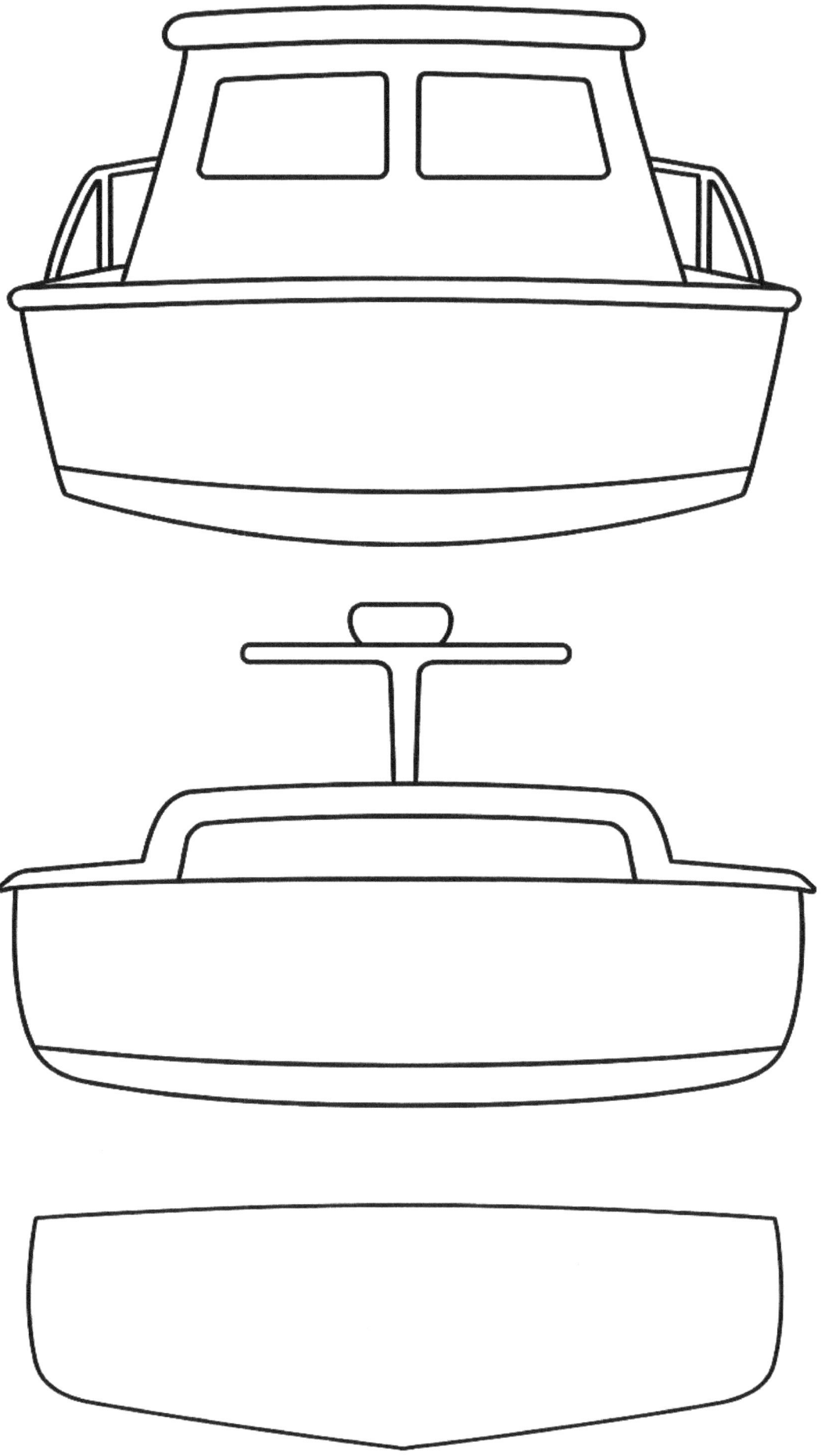

NOTES & DOODLES

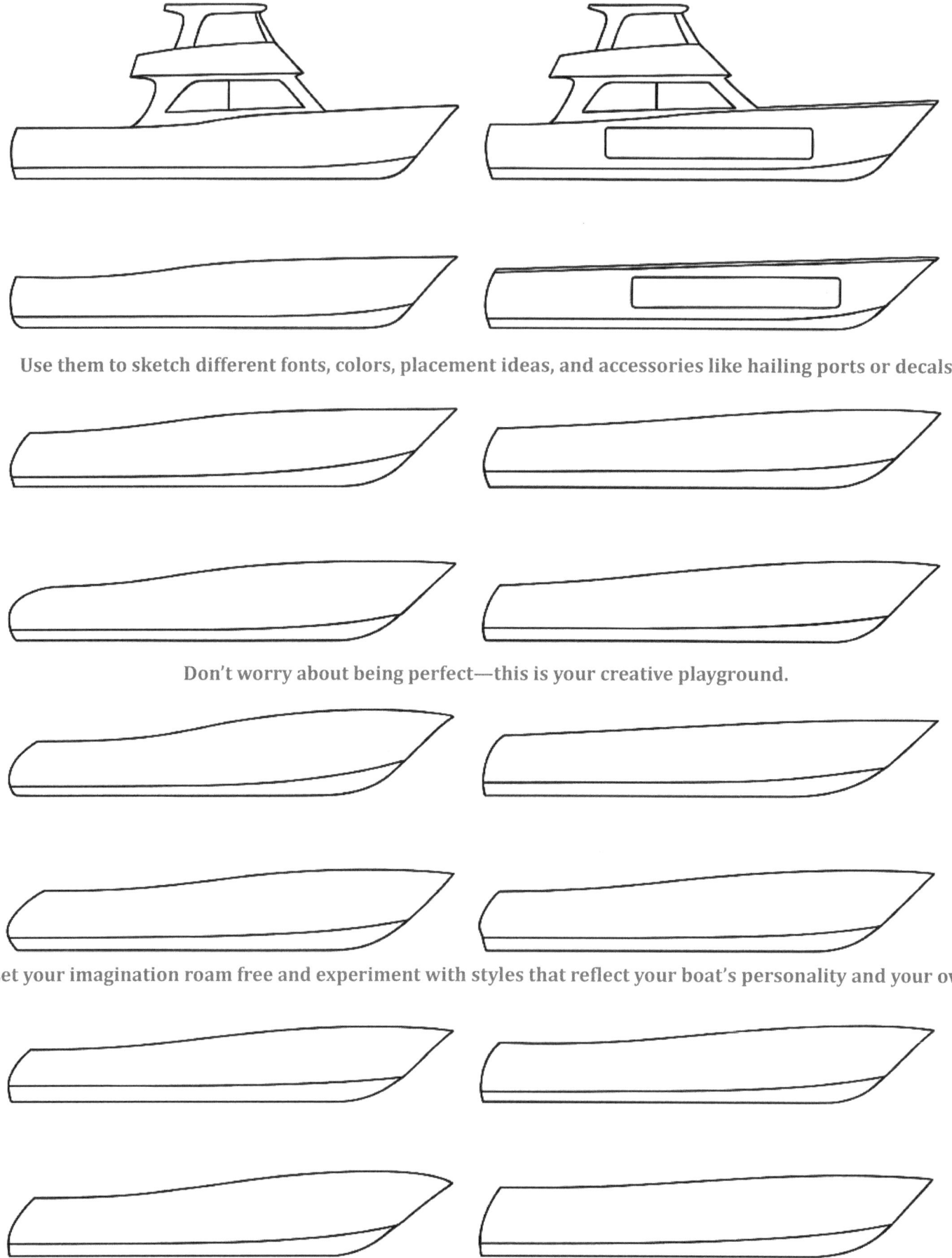

Use them to sketch different fonts, colors, placement ideas, and accessories like hailing ports or decals.

Don't worry about being perfect—this is your creative playground.

Let your imagination roam free and experiment with styles that reflect your boat's personality and your ow

NOTES & DOODLES

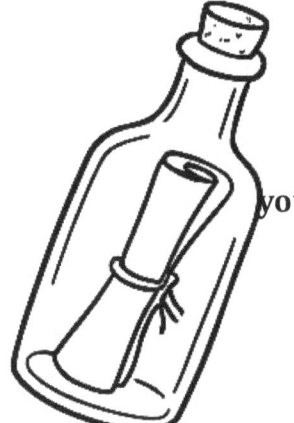

Thought of the perfect boat name?
Try it in *thesaurus.com*
you might discover an even cooler word
you hadn't considered!

Personalized Life Ring With Your Boat Name, Family Pool, Yacht

Looking for a meaningful gift for a boat owner or captain who has everything?
Custom life rings are the perfect blend of fun and function!
Add your boat's name, hailing port, or even a funny family phrase—
then let it ride the waves or hang proudly on the dock.
Each ring is weather-resistant, fully customizable, and made to order with
unlimited design proofs included.
A great gift for holidays, retirements, or just because!

New Jim-Buoy Life Ring
with Web Straps 24in. White.
Custom made Lettering and graphics.
Includes unlimited proofs
Via email.

Jim-Buoy Life Ring
with Web Straps!

20" White

Fully customizable text and design.
High-quality materials and professional printing.
Multiple color options to match their boat or theme.

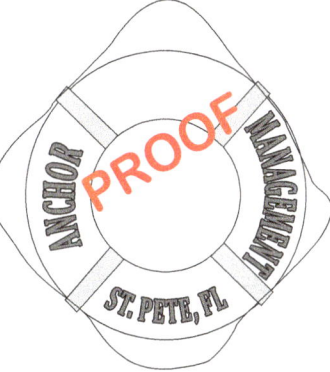

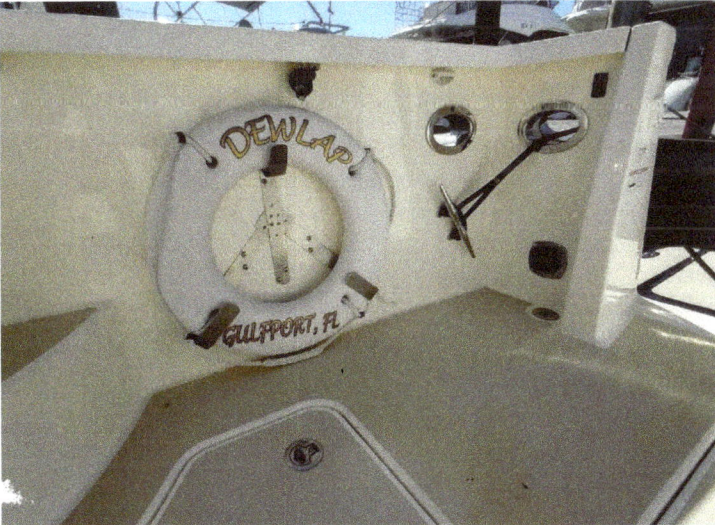

How to Order:
Fill out the boat name form as you would with a name but state you want a life ring. And note what size. 20" or 24"
I will return via email with a proof and estimate.

Let's create a gift they'll treasure for years to come!
Make this holiday unforgettable with a personalized gift that shows how much you care.
Order a Custom Life Ring today!

GO TO> >

**INTERESTED IN TIKI BAR SIGNS FOR YOUR BACK YARD OR DOCK??
GO TO TIKIBARSIGNS.COM**

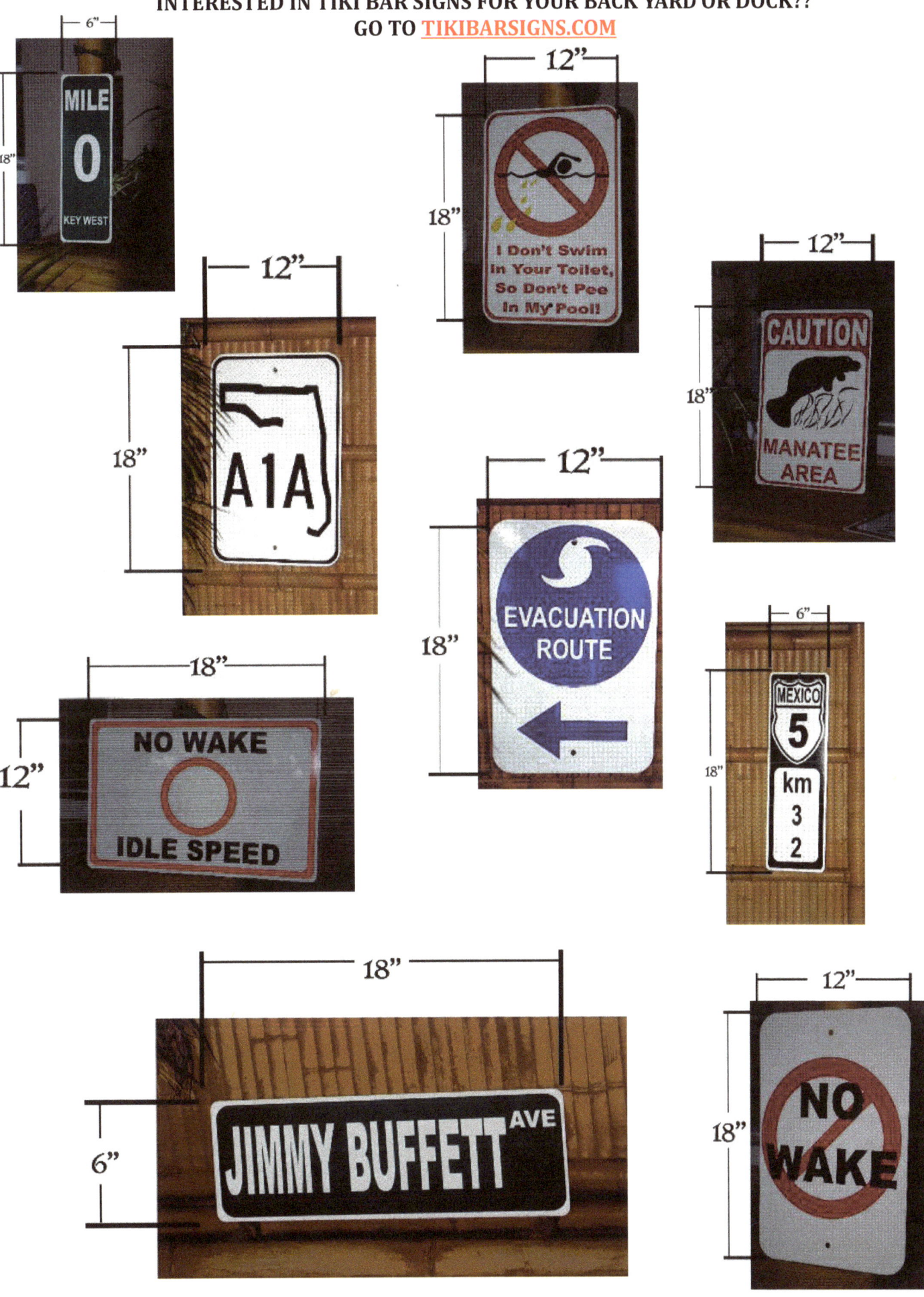

Give the Gift of a Boat Name — A Gift That Truly Makes Waves!

Finding the perfect gift for the boat lover in your life? Look no further.
A custom boat name gift certificate is the ultimate present for
any captain, first mate, or weekend warrior.
Whether it's for a birthday, retirement, Father's Day, Christmas, or a big
boat upgrade, this is more than just a gift
— it's a legacy on the water.
Let them name their vessel with confidence and style, with your
thoughtful contribution making it possible.

Why It Works:

Boat owners take pride in every detail of their vessel, and the name is the crown jewel.
With a gift certificate, you're giving them the freedom to personalize their boat name at their own pace
— with expert help just a message away.
It's perfect for new boaters, families, or those finally ready to rename an old friend.
Let them bring their story to life across the transom — and you'll be remembered every time they cast off.

BOAT NAME GIFT CERTIFICATES

 Pro Tip:

Surprise your spouse, friend, or parent with a custom boat name gift certificate for their engagement, birthday, or boat anniversary.
It's thoughtful, unique, and one they'll never forget
— because the name will be on display for years to come!

DONE-FOR-YOU INSTALLATION

Skip the sweat, skip the guesswork — I'll come to you.

Sure, you could send your design to a local sign shop or fire up a YouTube tutorial and try it yourself...
And if you've got the patience, the tools, and the confidence, I say go for it!
But if you're like most boaters I meet, you've already got enough projects to deal with. That's where I come in.

I offer mobile installation services — professionally prepped, leveled, and applied so your boat name looks perfect the first time. No bubbles. No crooked letters. No curse words shouted across the dock.

From idea to install, I handle it all so you can get back to boating.

I'm not here to make this book about me — this guide was made to help *anyone* bring their boat name to life. But if you decide you'd rather let someone else handle the sticky stuff, I've got your back (and your transom).

READY TO GET STARTED?

Scan the QR code below
or visit: **<u>boatnameguy.com/boat-name-form</u>**
to begin your custom boat name install today!

JUST NEED LETTERING?

Skip the custom design and get your boat name shipped, ready to install.
Visit my Etsy shop for easy-to-order lettering kits you can apply yourself —
great for DIYers or budget-minded boaters.

    Fast shipping
    Easy peel-and-stick application
    Just clean, position, and go!
Scan the QR code below to browse:

CHEEK PLAQUE RESTORATION

Before you toss those weathered plaques, consider this...

A lot of older boats still have their original cheek boards — those wooden plaques on either side of the bow — but after years of sun, salt, and neglect, they're often faded, cracked, or peeling. I bring them back to life.

From sanding and prep to sealing and new vinyl lettering, I take care of the full process. Whether you want to match the original look or give them a bold refresh, I'll make sure they look shipshape again.

The gallery here shows some recent before-and-after projects.
Each one gets:
- ✔ Gentle stripping and cleaning
- ✔ Custom-cut lettering
- ✔ Clear coat or varnish sealing
- ✔ Reinstallation with stainless fasteners (if needed)

Don't let great woodwork go to waste.
If you've got plaques like these that need a second life — reach out. I do this too.

20 COMMON WOOD SPECIES AND THEIR JANKA RATING

Rating (lbf)	Wood Species
3,684	IPE
3,220	EBONY
2,345	MESQUITE
1,980	BUBINGA
1,820	HICKORY
1,780	ROSEWOOD
1,630	WENGE
1,380	BAMBOO
1,360	WHITE OAK
1,320	ASH
1,290	RED OAK
1,155	TEAK
1,120	ENGLISH OAK
1,010	BLACK WALNUT
995	CHERRY
870	SOUTHERN YELLOW PINE
660	DOUGLAS FIR
540	POPLAR
410	BASSWOOD
380	EASTERN WHITE PINE

family handyman

SOME CUSTOM SIGNS CAN BE MADE IN AND AROUND YOUR BOAT

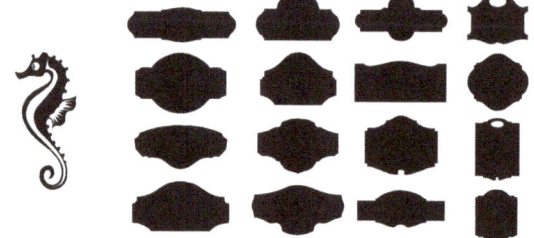

POOP DECK
NO SMOKING
SALTY DOG
SHOWER
PIRATES
HEAD
SKIPPER
SALTY DOG
SCREW ROOM

INTREPID: WHAT'S IN A NAME?

When naming new ships, the Secretary of the Navy often honors earlier vessels with distinguished service records. Four ships in the U.S. Navy have been named Intrepid, which means courageous or fearless.

The first Intrepid participated in the First Barbary War (1801–1805) between the United States and the Barbary States in North Africa. Built in France in 1798, the ship was a two-masted sailing vessel called a ketch.

The ship was sold to Tripoli and later captured by an American schooner in 1803. Taken into the U.S. Navy in 1804, the ship was re-named Intrepid and put under the command of Stephen Decatur. In February, Decatur and his crew sailed the Intrepid to Tripoli, boarded the captured American frigate Philadelphia, and burned that ship to keep her out of enemy hands. Later that year, the Intrepid was destroyed in an explosion in Tripoli.

Commissioned in 1874, the second Intrepid was an experimental steam torpedo ram. In 1882, the ship was decommissioned for conversion to a gunboat, but the work was never completed. The third Intrepid was commissioned in 1907 and served as a receiving ship, housing newly recruited sailors. The ship was decommissioned in 1921.
The aircraft carrier in which you are standing is the fourth U.S. Navy ship to carry the name Intrepid.

DID YOU KNOW?

Four U.S. Navy ships have proudly carried the name *Intrepid*,
meaning courageous or fearless.
The first? A captured ketch set ablaze in Tripoli by none other than
Stephen Decatur himself.
The fourth? You're standing on it — the legendary aircraft carrier
Intrepid, now retired and docked in NYC.

REAL NAMES. REAL BOATS.
REAL INSPIRATION.

Over the years, I've had the chance to bring hundreds of boat names to life — from bold and funny to clean and classy. What you'll see in the next few pages isn't about showing off… it's about **sparking ideas** for your own name and helping you picture how it might look in the real world.

These photos represent more than just vinyl — they tell stories. Some were inspired by a favorite song, others by a loved one, a lifestyle, or a good old-fashioned pun.

Take your time flipping through.
Notice the fonts, layouts, colors, and placement styles.
And ask yourself: *What direction do I want to go?*

You don't need to reinvent the ship — sometimes all it takes is seeing a name that makes you smile.

Let these pages help you find the vibe that fits your boat… and your story.

THE CAPTAIN'S COMPASS: SOLUTIONS TO PUZZLES

Nautical Know-How!

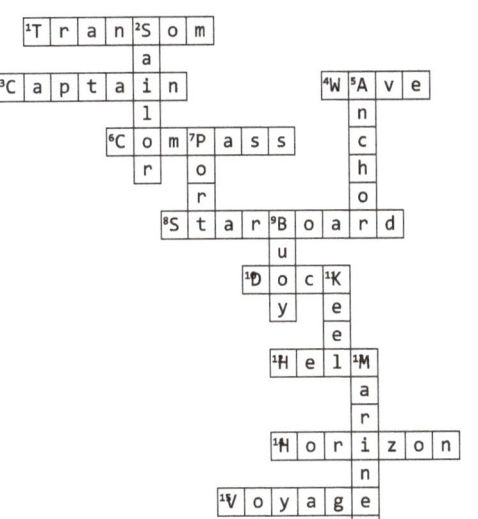

Anchors Away with Word Scrambles!

1. BOAT
2. SAIL
3. PIRATE
4. HOOK
5. WAVE
6. RAFT
7. HORN
8. JETTY
9. CANNON
10. MOTOR
11. STERN
12. COMPASS
13. FISH
14. YACHT
15. TIDE
16. LEDGE
17. NESTER
18. MARINA
19. FIN
20. LINE

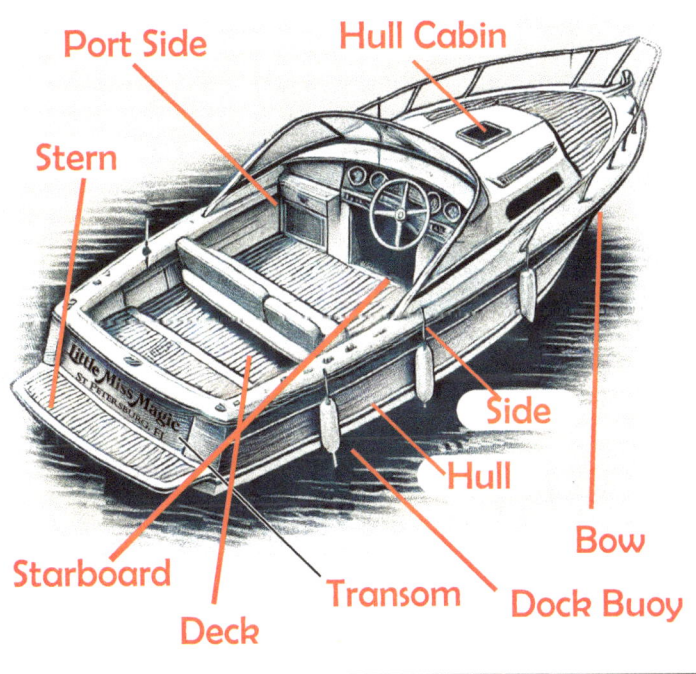

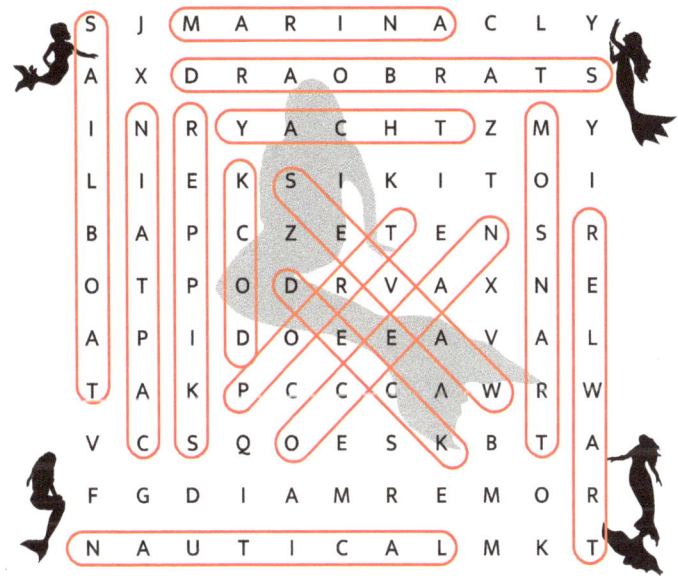

⚓ BOAT RULES

1. No shoes (unless they're white tennis shoes)

2. The Captain is always right

3. The boat doesn't run on Thank You's, but it might on beers

4. If the Captain is docking, sit down & SHUT UP

5. Put on a life jacket before you have a "Hold my beer" moment

6. If the Captain is wrong, refer to Rule # 2

Meet the Boat Name Guy & First Mate Lucy

Doug Rohloff, better known as *The Boat Name Guy* has been turning transoms into works of art for over 25 years.
Based in Florida, Doug has helped name and letter hundreds of boats, including more than ten docked at the prestigious Marriott Water Street Marina.

Whether you're looking for humor, elegance, or something deeply personal, Doug brings each boat name to life with style, creativity, and a designer's eye for detail.
From brainstorming and design to printing and installation, he's passionate about making sure your boat name reflects **you**.

By his side (or underfoot) is Lucy, his loyal 80-pound golden retriever and unofficial mascot. When she's not supervising installs or chasing seagulls, she keeps Doug company on long design days and even pops up in a few customer smiles.

Doug's real talent? Blending each boat owner's story, style, and spirit into something unforgettable.

Thanks for Reading

Thank you for spending time with this book — whether you're naming your first boat or your fifth,
I hope it brought some ideas, inspiration, and even a few laughs along the way.
If you enjoyed flipping through these pages,
just wait until you see what your boat name looks like out on the water.
Wishing you fair winds, smooth seas,
and a name you'll be proud of every time you set sail.

 — Doug & Lucy

www.ingramcontent.com/pod-product-compliance
Lightning Source LLC
Chambersburg PA
CBHW060940170426
43195CB00025B/2989